NESTBOXES FOR PRAIRIE BIRDS

BY MYRNA PEARMAN

ILLUSTRATED BY GARY ROSS

PUBLISHED BY

ELLIS BIRD FARM LTD.

BOX 2980, LACOMBE, ALBERTA

CANADA • T0C 1S0

PHONE: (403) 346-2211

C R E D I T S

First Edition

Canadian Cataloguing in Publication Data

Pearman, Myrna, 1956-
   Nestboxes for Prairie birds

   Includes index.
   ISBN 0-9694221-1-3

   1. Birdhouses.   2. Birds--Nests.   3. Birds,
Attracting of.   4. Birds--Prairie Provinces.
I. Ross, Gary, 1961-   II. Title.
QL676.5.P427 1992   639.9'7829712
                                  C92-091093-9

Cover Illustration:
Female Common Goldeneye by **Gary Ross**

PHOTOGRAPHY

Maurice Carlisle
Red-naped Sapsucker

Mark Degner
Northern Flicker, White-breasted Nuthatch

James R. Hill III
Purple Martin in gourd

Wolfgang Hoffman
Boreal Owl

Gordon Johnson
Black-capped Chickadee, Northern Saw-whet Owl fledgling, House Wren

Edgar T. Jones
Chestnut-backed Chickadee, Great Crested Flycatcher, Common Goldeneye, Hooded Merganser

Jim Messina/Prairie Wings
Western Bluebird, Wood Duck, Red-headed Woodpecker

Alan Nelson
Brown Creeper

Myrna Pearman
Mountain Bluebird, Boreal Chickadee, Boreal Chickadee nestlings, Northern Flicker nestlings, Northern Saw-whet Owl, Yellow-bellied Sapsucker, Tree Swallow, Pileated Woodpecker

Dick Peterson
Eastern Screech-Owl

Hardy Pletz
Northern Hawk Owl nestlings

Lorne Scott
American Kestrel

Tom Ulrich
Eastern Bluebird, Bufflehead, Mountain Chickadee, House Finch, Barrow's Goldeneye, Purple Martin at nestbox, Common Merganser, Red-breasted Nuthatch, Barred Owl, House Sparrow, Violet-green Swallow, Black-backed Woodpecker, Downy Woodpecker, Hairy Woodpecker, Three-toed Woodpecker

Jan Wassink
Northern Pygmy-Owl, European Starling, Cliff Swallow

Dan Wood
Burrowing Owl, Northern Hawk Owl

Photo of Charlie Ellis by **Myrna Pearman**; Photo of Lorne Scott by **Doug Gilroy**; Photo of John Lane and Brandon Junior Birders courtesy of Norah Lane

Author Photo by **Carolyn Sandstrom**

TABLE OF CONTENTS

INTRODUCTION AND ACKNOWLEDGMENTS

It was a warm morning in early April 1969, when my father rushed into the house to announce that a male Mountain Bluebird had landed on a tree beside him while he was repairing a pasture fence. It was the first bluebird he had seen since he and my mother had moved to a farm north of Rimbey, Alberta, in the early 1950s. He was so excited about seeing this beautiful bird that he packed the whole family into the old pickup and headed back to the field. Much to our disappointment, the elusive bluebird had disappeared.

Two years later, again in early April, a neighbor stopped by with a couple of bluebird nestboxes. He had just built them and thought we might be interested in setting them out. We accepted the boxes enthusiastically, and were rewarded the following spring with our first pair of bluebirds. Over the next few years, other neighbors started setting out boxes and it soon became evident that the bluebird population was responding favorably to our efforts. Today, we no longer screech to a halt when we notice a bluebird on a power line or at a nestbox. But, with each sighting, we feel a sense of satisfaction in knowing that we helped "bring back" this gentle harbinger of spring to our community.

Ours is a typical "bluebird story" — a story that has been repeated thousands of times across North America over the past half-century. Unlike condors and other such species whose fate depends on large budgets and highly skilled biologists, the needs of bluebirds and most other native cavity-nesting species can be significantly supported by ordinary people like you and me. Nestboxes, which provide the birds with critical housing, are relatively easy to construct, set out and monitor. Nestbox projects know no age, educational or socio-economic limits, and the level of commitment is up to each individual.

Now that this grassroots conservation movement has successfully re-established the bluebird in many parts of its former range, I hope the same remarkable effort will be carried through for our other native cavity nesters. This book is one small step towards that goal.

The information contained herein is a synthesis of my own experiences and research, as well as that of other researchers, ornithologists, backyard bird watchers and nestbox trail operators from across the continent. Some of the background information comes from a 1984 Ellis Bird Farm Ltd. publication, *Nestboxes For Alberta Birds*, by Bryan Shantz and Myrna Pearman.

I would like to take this opportunity to acknowledge the inspiration of my father, the late Philip Pearman, whose keen eye, wit and interest first sparked in me a love for wild places and wild creatures. To Fred Schutz, who took the time to answer the questions of a curious kid, and to Melvin Baumbach, who gave me my first bluebird box, thank you.

Deserving of special recognition for their support, patience and willingness to extend deadlines are the members of the board of directors of Ellis Bird Farm Ltd. Chairman Ken Larsen deserves special recognition for his unfailing encouragement, gentle prodding and red felt pen. Thanks also to the other board members: Winnie Ellis, Eldon Neufeld, Dell James, Fred Schutz, Howard Fredeen, Rick McConnell, Don Young and Orest Litwin.

The following experts provided up-to-date information on various species, for which I am grateful: ducks - Dr. Gilles Gauthier, Jim Potter, Dr. Jean-Pierre Savard; kestrels - Dr. Gary Bortolotti, Bill Iko; owls - Peter Boxall, Dr. Paul James, Ken de Smet, Colin Weir, Troy Wellicome, Dan and Gwen Wood; swallows - Dr. Peter Dunn, Cam Finlay, James R. Hill III, Charles McEwen; chickadees - Dr. Susan Hannon; wrens - Mike Quinn; bluebirds - Art Aylesworth, Elsie Elzroth, Earl Gillis, Duncan Mackintosh, Lorne Scott and Dr. Larry Zeleny.

I would also like to acknowledge members of the following bluebird organizations for their great contribution to bluebird conservation and for their willingness to share their expertise and experiences: Audubon Society of Corvallis Bluebird Trail, Bluebird Recovery Program of Minnesota, Bluebird Restoration Association of Wisconsin, Mountain Bluebird Trails, North American Bluebird Society, North Carolina Bluebird Society, Ohio Bluebird Society, and the producers of the *Bluebird News* (especially Keith Kridler and Robert McKinney).

I am indebted to Bob Kreba, Al Smith and Wayne Harris for providing information on Saskatchewan species, and to Jean Horton for providing the same for Manitoba. I would also like to acknowledge the following cast of talented birders, researchers and writers who have willingly shared with me their knowledge, experiences and editing abilities: Jim Allen, Vince Bauldry, Ted Code, Aaron Collins, Ross Dickson, Andre Dion, Dave Elphinstone, Louise Horstman, Dorothy Hill, Joe Huber, Mary and Dr. Stuart Houston, Dr. Dan Johnson, Gordon Johnson, Richard Klauke, Kathryn Kopciuk, Norah Lane, George Loades, Murray Mackay, Mike McNaughton, Dr. Martin McNicholl, Pat McIsaac, Sheryl Nixon, Verlyn Olson, Delbert Parkinson, Gelaine Pearman, Marie Pijeau, Jeff Pugh, Dr. Margo Pybus, Nora Ready, Jeff Smith, Harry Stelfox, Donald and Lillian Stokes, Joan Susut, Joanne Susut, Corinne Tastyre and Tom Webb. And for his special contribution to the editing, I gratefully acknowledge Dave Ealey.

Thanks also to the photographers, whose work is acknowledged on page 2, and to Gary Ross for the beautiful illustrations.

Last but not least, to Pat McVean, who generously donated her time and talent to this project, and who shared with me her enthusiasm and great sense of humor, thank you!

M. P.

Ellis Bird Farm Ltd. gratefully acknowledges the financial support of the Alberta Recreation, Parks and Wildlife Foundation.

Alberta, Saskatchewan and Manitoba make up the Canadian portion of the originally grass-covered interior plains of North America. Although only about one-third of the prairie provinces is actually classified as prairie, our well-known name comes from the vast area of grassland that stretched across the southern boundary of the three provinces. Much of the prairie has been cultivated, but there are still large tracts of this grassland that remain.

From east to west, the prairie provinces rise in a step-like fashion from the treeless tundra of the Hudson Plains in the northeast corner of Manitoba through to the towering and magnificent Rocky Mountains along the western edge of Alberta. Within these two extremes lie several broad ecozones, each of which in turn contains smaller units call ecoregions. The map below shows the broad vegetation zones that are associated with the major ecozones and ecoregions, based on the boundaries shown in Figure 1 of *Priority Migratory Bird Habitats of Canada's Prairie Provinces* by Poston et al. (1990, Canadian Wildlife Service).

This map illustrates regions that provide different habitats for various bird species. The species accounts will indicate which species can be expected in each region.

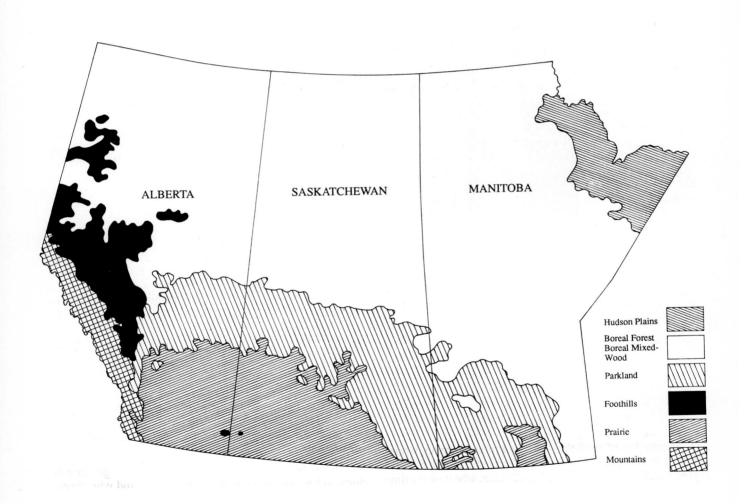

ALBERTA   SASKATCHEWAN   MANITOBA

Hudson Plains

Boreal Forest
Boreal Mixed-Wood

Parkland

Foothills

Prairie

Mountains

Cavity-nesting birds are unique among avian creatures because of their requirement for a hole or cavity in which to nest. Primary cavity-nesting birds, most notably the woodpeckers, have the remarkable ability to create their own cavities by excavating holes in tree trunks. Secondary cavity nesters also require cavities for nesting, but because they lack the adaptations necessary for the task of excavation, they rely on woodpeckers to create nesting sites for them. Secondary cavity nesters are not fussy tenants, so, in addition to old woodpecker holes, they will also nest in natural tree cavities, pockets in rock cliffs, holes in mud banks or a variety of human-made structures.

BIRDS AND FORESTS: A BENEFIT TO EACH OTHER

Among the most important sources of cavities for cavity-nesting birds are dead or deteriorating trees. Unfortunately, these trees are all too often cut down and removed because they are considered by landowners or forest managers to be unsightly, a danger to public safety or an impediment to efficient forest management.

A typical snag

While it is true that dead trees (called snags) or trees in varying stages of decay may lack the grandeur of their live counterparts, their role in the forest ecosystem is no less critical.

A host of wildlife species, from squirrels to birds, rely on them to provide both food and nesting sites. Birds also use them as perches for such activities as foraging, mating and singing.

The bird populations that are sustained by a forest ecosystem are its important allies because they play such a key role in the control of forest insect pests. Most cavity-nesting bird species are insectivorous, and because they make up a large proportion of the forest-dwelling bird population, their role in helping to maintain balanced and healthy forests cannot be underestimated.

In many cases, the nesting success of secondary cavity nesters is dependent on the number of cavities found in forest snags. For example, the Common Goldeneye typically uses old Pileated Woodpecker holes, while the smaller Bufflehead duck relies on cavities left by Northern Flickers. In most forested areas, these nesting sites are usually in short supply. This means that competition for nesting sites is fierce, not only between different species of cavity-nesting birds, but also between the birds and other wildlife species such as squirrels, mice, wasps, bees and ants.

FACTORS AFFECTING BIRD POPULATIONS

There are several factors that have an impact on the dynamics of wild bird populations. Factors such as drought, storms and cold periods on wintering areas are environmental events and totally beyond human control. Others, like pollution and the widespread alteration of habitat, are caused entirely by humans.

Although most human-related activities generally tend to have an adverse impact on most wildlife populations, the effects of habitat alteration have been favorable in some cases, unfavorable in others. In some areas, human settlement has actually increased and/or improved wildlife habitat for some species. On the prairies, for example, habitat for all cavity nesters has been increased because agricultural settlement has brought shelterbelt plantings and fire suppression—both of which have expanded the aspen parkland. Likewise, the opening up of forested areas has been beneficial for some species, especially bluebirds and other "edge" dwellers.

Where the original habitat has been removed to accommodate urban sprawl, monoculture farming or industrial developments, the impact has invariably been an adverse one and the only wildlife species, if any, that benefit are the more tolerant and adaptable.

We have dealt cavity-nesting birds a "double whammy" because, in addition to the problems created for other wildlife, we have added for these birds the burden of competition from exotic species. In the mid- and late 1800s, House Sparrows and European Starlings, both secondary cavity nesters, were introduced into North America from Europe. They became successfully established soon after their introduction, and their populations increased at an explosive rate throughout the continent. These aggressive, intelligent and persistent competitors have compounded the problem of habitat loss, and have played a large role in thwarting efforts both to bring native species back to traditional nesting areas and to introduce them into newly created, suitable habitat.

HELPING CAVITY NESTERS WITH NESTBOXES

Fortunately, most species of secondary cavity-nesting birds will readily accept a nestbox or other "artificial" cavity in which to build their nest. Because of this, many species, especially bluebirds, have benefited from the efforts of concerned individuals and groups who have established nestbox trails for them. A nestbox "trail" simply consists of a number of nestboxes set out along a prescribed route. It is important to note that only cavity-nesting bird species will be attracted to nestboxes. Most birds, including such backyard birds as hummingbirds, jays or goldfinches will not be attracted to nest in a nestbox.

Before European colonization of North America, native American Indians attracted Purple Martins to their villages by setting out hollowed-out gourds similar to that shown below. Today, martins rely almost entirely on human-made structures for nesting, and are welcome visitors into the backyards of Purple Martin "landlords" throughout the continent. Organizations dedicated to Purple Martin conservation are listed on page 48.

Thomas E. Musselman of Illinois, USA, is generally credited with being the originator of a regional bluebird conservation program and for coining the term "bluebird trail." Beginning in 1926, he encouraged widespread public participation in bluebird conservation. Since that time, there have been numerous others who have spearheaded projects involving up to thousands of nestboxes and the participation of hundreds of people. The first organization dedicated entirely to the restoration of bluebird populations, the North American Bluebird Society, was founded in 1978 by Dr. Lawrence Zeleny of Maryland, USA. Today, there are many regional bluebird groups in both Canada and the United States. For a list of these groups, see page 63 or contact Ellis Bird Farm Ltd. for a copy of the *North American Bluebird Trail Directory*.

More recently, kestrels and ducks have also become the focus of conservation efforts. Kestrel Karetakers, founded in 1975 by Roger Jones of Virginia, USA, is an organization that encourages the use of kestrel nestboxes (see page 27). Many individuals, along with Ducks Unlimited and government fish and wildlife agencies, actively promote cavity-nesting duck conservation.

With the exception of those for Burrowing Owls, nestbox programs for owls have been more informal than those for other secondary cavity nesters. Several Albertans who have set up their own nestbox trails have been successful in attracting Saw-whet owls .

Purple Martin at a gourd nest

Saw-whet Owl fledgling

Although bluebirds and other secondary cavity nesters no doubt took advantage of the gourd nest sites, the earliest written account of bluebirds using nestboxes was by Henry David Thoreau, who noted in his September 29, 1842 diary that bluebirds visited his "boxes."

In Canada, most provinces have groups or individuals who are actively involved in the conservation of native cavity-nesting birds, especially bluebirds. Some provinces also have government programs that encourage the use of nestboxes as wildlife management tools.

In addition to the large, organized trails and groups listed below, thousands of people across Canada maintain nestbox trails around their farms and communities. These more informal trails are not always extensive, but their contribution has been, and will continue to be, very significant.

BRITISH COLUMBIA

Although there have been active nestbox trail operators in BC for several years, the first effort to collect province-wide data on bluebird nestbox trails was undertaken in 1990 by Harold Pollock of Victoria.

Nestbox trails are located as far north as Smithers, with other large trails found around Williams Lake, Kamloops, Kelowna, Penticton, Kimberly, Castlegar, Princeton, Cranbrook and Grand Forks. The largest trail in the province (over 700 boxes) is operated by Vern Johnson of Oliver.

Some trail operators in the southeastern part of the province belong to the Mountain Bluebird Trails group (see Alberta).

ALBERTA

The first large-scale bluebird conservation program in Alberta was undertaken by Charles Ellis and his sister Winnifred of Lacombe. The story of the Ellises and Ellis Bird Farm Ltd. is outlined on the inside front cover.

Charlie Ellis - "Mr. Bluebird"

In 1971, Joy and Cam Finlay started a bluebird nestbox trail in the Edmonton area with a group of young naturalists. When the Edmonton Natural History Club became involved in 1972, the group assumed maintenance of this trail and started new ones to the west of the city. Other large trails were started in 1971 by Edgar T. Jones and Ken Trann in the Cooking Lake area and by Jack Kinnaird west of Barrhead.

Pres Winter of Viking and the Castor Fish and Game Association also set up extensive trails in the 1970s. The first large-scale production and distribution of bluebird boxes in Alberta started when Horace Ramsell built 3,000 boxes in 1974. Since that time, about 50,000 boxes have been distributed by the John Janzen Nature Centre in Edmonton.

Harold Pinel started a nestbox trail in the Calgary area in the early 1970s; it now consists of more than 2,000 boxes and is maintained by the Calgary Field Naturalists' Society under the direction of Don Stiles and Jean Moore.

In 1992, Alberta Government Telephones (AGT) launched a program, called Feather Care, to convert their canister-type buried cable markers into nestboxes. Contact Brian Cowan (AGT, 10020-100 St., Edmonton, AB T5J 0N5) or your regional AGT office for more information on this program.

Jim Potter of Red Deer has pioneered efforts in Alberta to assist cavity-nesting ducks. With the help of his brother Steve, and most recently through his work with Alberta Fish and Wildlife, Jim has set out more than 600 duck nestboxes.

Eva Dannacker of Edmonton, known as the "Purple Martin Lady", has been Alberta's most enthusiastic promoter of Purple Martins.

Burrowing Owl conservation in Alberta, which has been carried out through the efforts of individuals, government wildlife agencies and conservation groups, is described on page 33.

SASKATCHEWAN

Lorne Scott of Indian Head first started building bluebird boxes in 1963, when he was a grade 10 student. He added approximately 200 boxes to his trail each year, and by 1975 had a 960-km (600-mi.) route of over 2,000 boxes. His trail extended from Regina Beach in the west, Broadview in the east, Melville to the northeast and Raymore to the northwest. In 1968, his trail was linked up with the Brandon Junior Birders' trail at Broadview.

Lorne Scott, 1969

Stuart and Mary Houston of Saskatoon, together with Ray Bisha, started an extensive trail around Saskatoon in the late 1960s.

Their trail extended from Langham in the west to Raymore in the east, where it connected with Lorne Scott's trail. Jake Kargut continued the western portion of the trail to Denholm.

In 1985, the Saskatchewan Natural History Society (SNHS) and the Saskatchewan Telephone Pioneers started a cooperative nestbox project. Volunteers with the Telephone Pioneers, a service-oriented group of former telephone company employees, have been making nestboxes out of old switch covers. These boxes are distributed through members of the SNHS. By the end of 1991, more than 5,000 boxes had been constructed and distributed.

Shirley McKercher of Saskatoon started a nestbox trail program in 1986. With the assistance of 24 volunteers, she now oversees a trail of approximately 1,200 boxes.

Saskatchewan has an extensive Burrowing Owl conservation program, described on page 33.

MANITOBA

Bluebird conservation in Manitoba began with Jack and Norah Lane who started the Brandon Junior Birders nature club in 1958. They first started setting out boxes in 1960 and expanded their trail annually until 4,500 boxes extended over some 2,560 km (1,600 mi.) from the International Peace Gardens in the south, Elm Creek in the east, Ste. Rose du Lac in the north and west to Broadview, where they linked up with the Saskatchewan trails. At Elm Creek, they joined a line from Winnipeg built by Louis Brown and his students. Other trails in the Morden, Selkirk and Winnipeg areas were also started.

The result of this massive effort for bluebird conservation in Saskatchewan and Manitoba, which included side trails operated by conservation clubs, scout groups and natural history organizations, was the largest bluebird trail in the world—7,000 boxes spread out across 4,000 km (2,500 mi.)!

Shortly after Jack Lane's death in 1975, an organization, Friends of the Bluebirds, was formed to ensure that his pioneering efforts were carried on. Today, under the guidance of Ann Smith, the group has 100 monitors who look after about 3,500 nestboxes.

Purple Martin conservation in Manitoba has been spearheaded by the Manitoba Purple Martin Club under the direction of Ernie Didur.

A Burrowing Owl conservation program has been underway in Manitoba for several years and is described on page 33.

ONTARIO

The Oshawa Naturalists Club, the Willow Beach Field Naturalist Club and the Ontario Bird Banding Association have established extensive nestbox trails in southern Ontario. Today, the Ontario Eastern Bluebird Society, founded and headed by William Read, is the most active group in the province. The objectives of the society are to increase the number of managed nestbox trails in Ontario, to give expertise or guidance to new trail operators and to monitor bluebird population trends in Ontario.

Long Point Bird Observatory and the Ontario Ministry of Natural Resources promote the use of duck nestboxes, and sponsored a duck box survey in 1990 and 1991.

QUEBEC

France and André Dion of St. Placide have pioneered efforts to bring the bluebird back to Quebec. In addition to operating a nestbox trail and producing books about bluebirds, the Dions also founded the Société des Amis du Merle Bleu de L'Est de L'Amérique in 1986.

Three other groups, the Société d'Animation Scientifique Québec Inc., the Association des amateurs d'hirondelles du Québec and the Comité de Conservation du Merle-Bleu de L'Est, are also active in promoting the conservation of native cavity-nesting birds throughout the province.

MARITIMES

A bluebird trail set up in New Brunswick by the Moncton Naturalists' Club is now maintained by interested individuals.

The Purple Martin and Bird Society of South Eastern New Brunswick is dedicated to the conservation of all birds, especially swallows. Charles McEwen has been very active in Purple Martin research and conservation.

YUKON

The Department of Renewable Resources has been actively promoting bluebird conservation in the Yukon since the mid-1980s. Most trails are cared for by school children and scout groups.

John Lane and the Brandon Junior Birders, 1970

The success of a nestbox trail depends on the factors summarized in this section. With thousands of people now operating successful trails throughout North America, new ideas, discoveries and techniques seem to come to light on a weekly basis. We have attempted to include most field-proven innovations or tips relevant to the prairies, but acknowledge there may still be others. If you have had success with a design, idea or technique not mentioned here, we would appreciate you sharing it with us.

BREEDING POPULATIONS AND HABITAT REQUIREMENTS

The distribution, ecology and habitat requirements vary for each species of bird. Before setting out boxes or planning a nestbox trail, the range, relative abundance and habitat of each species should be generally known. It would be unrealistic, for example, to expect Mountain Chickadees to use nestboxes on trails in Saskatchewan or Manitoba, or for bluebirds to use boxes placed in dense coniferous forests. There is the possibility, however, that a species not normally nesting in an area will be attracted to a nestbox. If you find an unusual nestbox occupant, contact your local nature centre, conservation group or one of the organizations named in the Resource File (page 75).

NESTBOX CONSTRUCTION AND DESIGN

We have all seen those wonderful "doll house" bird houses in magazines and woodworking books. Like miniature Edwardian mansions, they are wonderfully ornate and often complete with gabled roofs, balconies and elaborate scrolled woodwork. Unfortunately, these "bird houses" are more a tribute to craftsmanship than ecology and some may even be detrimental to the birds they are intended to help.

Nestboxes should be designed with function and durability, not artistry, in mind. Over decades, dozens of box styles have been developed and are being used successfully throughout North America. Of course, every trail operator will argue the merits of his or her own particular design and friendly debate over the perfect nestbox will forever rage!

DRAINAGE. Openings for drainage should be provided in the floor. The recommended method is to cut 19 mm (3/4 in.) diagonally away from each corner of the bottom board. Another technique is to drill 10-mm (3/8-in.) drainage holes directly into the floor board.

The floor should be recessed about 6 mm (1/4 in.) up from the bottom of the sides to help prevent moisture deterioration.

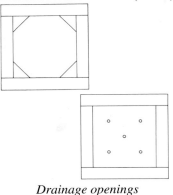

Drainage openings

ENTRANCE HOLES. Entrance hole sizes are of critical importance, and on smaller boxes should never exceed 40 mm (1 9/16 in.). Anything larger will admit starlings. On small boxes (except those for Purple Martins—see page 44-49), the top of the entrance hole should be 5 cm (2 in.) below the top of the front panel. On large boxes, it should be 7.6-10 cm (3 - 4 in.).

Entrance holes can be drilled in the smaller boxes with a spade or expandible drill bit, a hole saw or a Forstner-type drill bit. The last two leave the cleanest cut. If you are fussy, you can then take a router with a 6-mm (1/4-in.) quarter-round bit and router around the entrance hole to leave a very smooth finish and remove all sharp edges and splinters. Entrance holes on larger boxes should be cut out with a jig saw.

EXIT AIDS. Shallow saw slashes (saw kerfs) should be made on the inside of the front panel to help the fledglings exit the box. A piece of hardware cloth or small ribs of wood serve the same purpose.

FINISHING. While not essential, staining or painting a box will improve its appearance and add years of life to it. Chemical wood preservatives should be avoided. Exterior (no lead) paint or stain should be applied to the exterior of the box. The interior of the box and exposed rim of the entrance hole should not be painted. Subdued colors, such as dull gray, green or brown, are inconspicuous and less likely to invite vandalism. In southern areas, light colors should be used since dark-colored boxes tend to increase the internal box temperature. A linseed oil treatment will also preserve the box. The oil reacts with oxygen to form a tough, hard coating which will not vaporize or harm the birds.

MATERIALS. It makes good environmental sense to use scrap lumber wherever possible to build nestboxes. Lumber yards and building sites are often good sources of scrap lumber.

The ideal materials to use for nestbox construction are 19-mm (3/4-in.) exterior grade fir plywood or cedar boards. Exterior grade spruce plywood is also widely used. Thick wood provides good insulation against early spring chills and summer heat while thinner material provides less insulation and deteriorates sooner. Spruce boards tend to crack and shrink, so should be avoided. Pressure-treated lumber may contain harmful chemicals, so should not be used.

Wood glue used in addition to nails will make the boxes stronger, though porcupines may be attracted to the glue and chew the box.

Box longevity will be increased if galvanized or cement coated nails, which are rust-resistant, are used. Larger boxes should be assembled using wood screws, drywall screws or rust-proof deck screws instead of nails.

Milk cartons, plastic jugs and tin cans are sometimes converted into nestboxes. Milk cartons should never be used because they are too light and deteriorate too quickly. Boxes made from plastic and tin are usually less than optimal because they provide little insulation against temperature extremes. It should be noted that, before the widespread use of wooden nestboxes on the prairies, metal twine boxes on grain binders provided important nesting sites for bluebirds and other small cavity nesters. Plastic nestboxes are used by Ducks Unlimited for Wood Ducks, but these have not yet been field tested for suitability in northern regions.

For those who prefer to make more "natural" nestboxes, several options are available. If you happen upon a fallen tree containing a woodpecker cavity or natural cavity, cut it to an appropriate length and convert the hollow section into a nestbox by attaching a plywood lid and floor. You could also try contacting your local, professional tree-trimming company to see if they would save tree sections containing cavities for you. These "boxes" can then be wired to trees.

If you have proficiency with a chain saw, you can create a cavity in a standing dead tree. Cut a series of vertical, then horizontal cuts into the back of the tree, then extract the pieces. Drill an appropriately sized entrance hole into the front of the cavity, and seal up the back with plywood.

Slab lumber with the bark still attached, found at saw mills, can be used to make rustic-looking boxes. Cut the slabs to standard inside dimensions and allow for their varying thickness.

Log boxes can also be made by using a large Forstner-type bit to drill out a cavity in a section of a tree trunk. Although these bits are very expensive, and a large lathe or vertical milling machine is needed to power them, they enable you to make very attractive and functional nestboxes.

Nestbox Numbering. Boxes should be numbered sequentially along your trail. Numbers can be placed on the inside or outside of the box, or both. Large numbers on the outside of the box serve to identify it clearly. Paint and waterproof pens tend to fade quickly unless the number is placed under the roof overhang and renewed periodically. Some trail operators use metal house numbers while others cut out number shapes from plastic bleach or antifreeze bottles.

Opening Panels. Boxes should always be constructed so that one panel (front, top or side) opens easily to provide for observation, cleaning and removal of pests. Top-opening styles cause less disturbance to the occupants, are better for

banding and photography, and if they have removable floors are just as easy to clean out as the side- or front-opening styles. Side- and front-opening styles make checking for nest parasites easier, can be mounted higher, last longer in pastures where cattle tend to rub the boxes, and are easier to construct.

Perches. Perches should not be put on the front of small nestboxes because they assist House Sparrows and predators to enter. On duck boxes, a small wooden block can be mounted below the entrance hole. This "perch" makes it easier for the female duck to squeeze into the entrance hole.

Perching sites adjacent to bluebird nestboxes will be used regularly. If boxes are placed along fencelines, mount the box so it faces the next post or a nearby single tree. For boxes placed out in open areas, artificial perches can be made from small saplings or from 2-m (6-ft.) high posts with dowelling fastened horizontally to the top of them. They should be placed anywhere between 1 m and 10 m (3 - 30 ft.) in front of the box.

Roof. The roof should slope towards the front of the box with an overhang extending at least 5 cm (2 in.). The overhang protects the entrance hole from driving rains and casts a shadow over the entrance hole, thus helping keep the box cool on hot days. In areas where predators are a problem, the roof should have an even larger overhang (at least 10 cm [4 in.]) to discourage their access to the entrance hole. Covering the roof with an asphalt shingle, trimmed to size, will weather-proof it.

Ventilation. Three 10-mm (3/8-in.) holes for ventilation should be provided near the top of each side board. If the holes are drilled on an upward angle, they will provide ventilation without allowing rain to blow in. Vent holes should be placed above the level of the entrance hole to prevent a draft on the nestlings. It has been suggested that ventilation holes will also allow light into the box, enabling the bird to determine whether or not the box is safe to enter, especially when first prospecting for boxes in the fall or early spring.

Ventilation slots can also be provided on front- and side-opening boxes by leaving a space between the top of the pivoting panel and the roof.

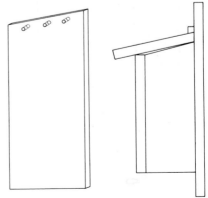

Ventilation holes and slots

NESTBOX PLACEMENT

The selection of appropriate locations and habitats for nestboxes is as important as the design of the box. The following ideas should be used as basic guidelines. Specific suggestions about placement are given at the conclusion of each species discussion.

You should always obtain permission from landowners before placing boxes. The courtesy of keeping the landowners informed of the productivity of your boxes on their property may encourage them to become involved. If you plan to set up a nestbox trail in a park or other protected area, be sure to consult with the park managers first; some parks do not allow nestboxes, especially in wilderness areas.

Box size, habitat and the potential for predator problems will determine where, how and to what you mount your boxes. Fenceposts are most commonly used for the smaller species, while trees are usually used for the larger species. Boxes can also be mounted on free-standing wooden or metal posts. Some trail operators have even designed boxes that hang from wire strung between two high posts, or on a barbed wire fence midway between fenceposts. Wooden Purple Martin houses, because of their weight and height above the ground, require a special mounting structure (see page 49).

Fencelines around pastures and in appropriate habitat along highways and secondary roads are convenient places to set up trails for bluebirds, wrens and swallows, but some mortality of fledglings can be expected where boxes are placed along well-travelled roads. Boxes set out along highways should face parallel, rather than at right angles to the road. The young birds will then be more likely to take their first flight along the ditch, rather than across the path of an oncoming automobile. Some trail operators report less vandalism along busy highways than quieter country roads. Fencelines beneath power line wires are ideal for bluebirds, since high wires are often used as sighting perches for foraging. If boxes are placed around a pasture, they should be placed on the outside of the fence, because domestic animals may rub them if they are placed pasture-side.

Boxes can be attached to support structures using various techniques, some of which are shown at right. If fenceposts are used, boxes should be attached using nails, screws, lag bolts or a wrap of wire. The advantage of using screws or lag bolts is that the box can be removed without damage. Boxes attached by a wrap of wire are less easily rubbed off than those secured only by nails.

Some trail operators have found that, in areas where wildlife are abundant, box survival will be increased if the box is attached only at the top. If it is bumped into by an animal, it will tend to swing rather than break apart. Horses are especially adept at chewing nestboxes, so boxes placed around horse pastures should be mounted on metal posts or conduit out of their reach. They can be discouraged from rubbing on posts by wrapping the posts with barbed wire.

In areas where predators may be a problem, boxes should be mounted on free-standing posts. Wooden posts, metal posts, galvanized pipe, rebar, U-posts, conduit and PVC pipe can all be used. Wooden or metal posts can simply be pounded into the ground while thinner materials should be attached to a fencepost or other sturdy base. Combination base and sleeve structures, shown at the bottom left, can also be used. The base post should be mounted permanently in the ground. If the sleeve post is slightly larger than the base post, it can slip over the post and can be held in place at the desired height by inserting bolts or nails through holes that have been predrilled through both posts. If the sleeve post is slightly smaller, it can be slipped inside the base post and held at the desired height by using a bolt or nail stopper. When the stopper is removed, the sleeve post can be lowered for box inspection or cleanout.

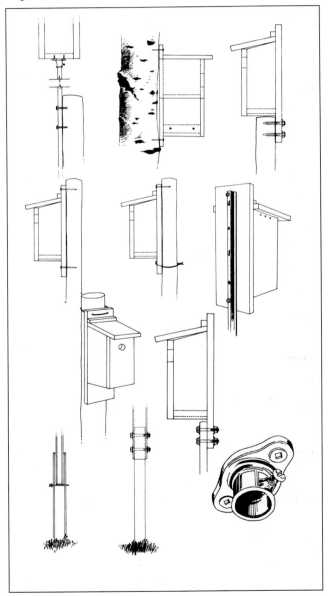

Mounting nestboxes

Boxes can be mounted on free-standing posts using wire or bolts. They can also be attached using a 1.2-cm (1/2-in.) pipe plate (also called floor flange) that has been fitted with a conduit sleeve (see bottom right of illustration).

Trees provide ideal locations for mounting owl, duck and kestrel boxes. They may have to be predator-proofed. Large boxes attached to trees should be secured with spikes or lag bolts. The advantage of lag bolts is that they can be loosened periodically to allow for tree growth. Boxes should be attached so that they tilt slightly forward, making it easier for the young to climb up the inside. Because of their frail condition, dead trees should not be used for mounting boxes.

Although utility poles would make excellent mounting posts, utility companies in most areas strictly prohibit their use in this way. Please respect this restriction.

Church-yards, cemeteries and golf courses are often chosen for setting up nestbox trails. Although they may provide ideal habitat, the risk associated with these areas is that they are usually subjected to heavy and continual applications of pesticides and herbicides. There are many documented cases of birds dying after commercial lawn applications of these toxic chemicals.

Nest orientation is not of critical importance to the birds, though some small cavity nesters seem to prefer boxes that face in an easterly direction. The larger cavity nesters apparently show no preference. Over heating, which is often a problem in southern latitudes, is not usually a problem as far north as the prairies. We are more often faced with the opposite problem of cold, wet weather. To minimize the amount of rain that might blow into a box during inclement weather, try to face the entrance hole away from the direction of the prevailing wind.

NESTBOX MONITORING AND MAINTENANCE

A small nestbox trail, properly managed, is much better than a large number of boxes set out and left unattended. Boxes that are set out and then ignored end up falling into disrepair or are more typically taken over by undesirable species. A nestbox that raises sparrows or starlings is worse than no box at all. Even if desirable birds continue to use the box, nesting material will build up dangerously close to the entrance hole, unnecessarily exposing the nest occupants to predators.

Checking your boxes on a regular basis will enable you to monitor nesting activity and keep accurate records of productivity. Initial box inspections should take place in mid-March to ensure that the boxes are ready for their intended occupants. The frequency of monitoring required during the nesting season varies between species, because some are more tolerant of frequent disturbance than others.

Most cavity-nesting species are especially sensitive to disturbance during two stages of the breeding cycle: females may abandon the nest if disturbed during the first stages of incubation, and nestlings may leave the nest prematurely if disturbed within a few days of fledging—see species descriptions for more details.

For the smaller species, weekly monitoring is sufficient to keep track of nesting progress yet minimize unnecessary disturbance. Once the birds are feeding young, monitoring can be more frequent. To monitor a box occupied by small cavity nesters, approach while making soft noises to warn the female of your presence. Lightly tap the side of the box, then quietly and slowly open it. When you have finished a brief observation, close the box and leave quietly. Of course, boxes should never be monitored during inclement weather.

Ducks are quite sensitive to disturbance, so should be monitored only occasionally. Kestrels and owls seem to be less sensitive than ducks, but regular monitoring should begin only after you are sure that they have been incubating for at least two weeks. More details about monitoring are included in the species descriptions.

You will observe that the nests of the smaller cavity nesters remain free of feces until the nestlings are almost ready to fledge. This is because the waste material of the young is encased in small mucous sacs. The parents carry these fecal sacs out of the nest and deposit them a safe distance from the nest. In addition to being sanitary, this practice makes the nest less likely to be found by predators.

After the young have fledged, nestboxes occupied by the smaller cavity nesters should be cleaned out. This prevents the nesting material from building up close to the entrance hole and helps control nest parasites. There is some evidence to suggest that nestbox trail operators can help increase the population of jewel wasps, which are natural predator of blowflies, by either collecting nests or by leaving them in the box over winter. See page 17 for more details.

When cleaning a nestbox, be careful to avoid inhaling the dust that is contained in the nesting material: it may contain high nitrate fecal material and harmful bacteria.

Duck, owl and kestrel boxes do not have to be cleaned out every year, though a fresh supply of shavings should usually be added.

In the fall, cleaned-out boxes should be converted to "non-cavities" for the winter to keep out unwanted tenants. The easiest way to do this is to seal up the entrance hole with a plug, duct tape or cover it with a block of wood. To discourage sparrow use, a small block of wood with a 25-mm (1-in.) hole in it can be tacked over the entrance hole. The sparrows may inspect the box, but upon finding the hole too small will likely not bother it further. If your boxes have removable floors, they should be tipped up against the back of the box. Some nestbox trail operators remove the lids for the winter. Although this will prevent the boxes from being used, it will also hasten their deterioration.

KEEPING RECORDS

Keeping accurate records of the location, occupants, and successes or failures in each nestbox is important. The records need not be detailed, but should be collected consistently from year to year. The manner in which records are collected can vary according to the preference of the individual monitor. Some trail operators use standardized forms while others jot notes down in notebooks or small binders. The recording forms shown below are an example of data that can be collected. You may want to photocopy and use this page for your field forms.

Annual summaries of nestbox trail data can be submitted to your local nature centre, conservation organization, Ellis Bird Farm Ltd. or to the Prairie Nest Record Card Scheme, c/o Manitoba Museum of Man and Nature, 190 Rupert Ave., Winnipeg, MB R3B 0N2.

Some of the terms commonly used when keeping records are explained here. HABITAT: used to describe the area surrounding the box, such as grassland, hayfield, forage crop, cereal crop (specific crops may be described), summerfallow, stream bank, mixed-wood forest, coniferous forest, deciduous forest, shrubland, badlands, acreage (no farm buildings), farmyard, urban yard, urban park, golf course, cemetery, lake or pond side or other. BOX HEIGHT: the distance between the bottom of the entrance hole and the ground. MOUNTED ON: fencepost, pipe, tree, etc. FLOOR SIZE: the total floor area. HOLE SIZE: diameter of the entrance hole. ASPECT: the direction the hole faces.

RECORDING FORM

Year _____ Nestbox Number _____

Landowner_____

Location _____1/4 of S____T_____R_____W of_____Mer.

Habitat _____

_____

Box Height_____ Mounted On_____

Floor Size_____ Hole Size_____ Aspect_____

	First	Second
Species		
# Eggs		
#Hatched		
#Fledged		
Hatch Date		

_____

_____

_____

_____

RECORDING FORM

Year _____ Nestbox Number _____

Landowner_____

Location _____1/4 of S____T_____R_____W of_____Mer.

Habitat _____

_____

Box Height_____ Mounted On_____

Floor Size_____ Hole Size_____ Aspect_____

	First	Second
Species		
# Eggs		
#Hatched		
#Fledged		
Hatch Date		

_____

_____

_____

_____

Even the most diligently tended trails have occasional problems. Many problems arise because of the design or nestbox location and can be easily dealt with, while others are the result of factors beyond the control of either the birds or the trail operator. The following are some of the major problems that may be encountered on a nestbox trail.

ABANDONMENT

In many bird species, the female alone does the incubating and if she is killed, the young will die before hatching. In some cases, however, it is possible to "foster" out abandoned eggs to other nests of the same species. Fostering should be attempted only if the stage of incubation of the abandoned eggs is known to match that of the foster clutch. This is a good reason for keeping careful records! It is not true that touching the eggs or nest will cause the birds to abandon—most birds have a very poorly developed sense of smell.

Unlike incubation, feeding and caring for the young is usually shared by both parents (except for ducks, because the males abandon their mates during incubation). If one parent is killed, the other one can successfully feed and fledge the brood. For this reason, nestlings can be considered abandoned only if they are obviously weak or if it is known that both parents are dead. If they are too weak to lift their heads or open their mouths, the chances of them surviving are slight. If, however, they are strong enough to open their mouths, they will likely survive if they can be fostered out to another set of parents. Ideally, another nest containing young of the same species at exactly the same age or slightly younger than the foster baby can be located. Unless their own clutch is unusually small, each pair of foster parents should be given only one orphan. Since ducklings remain in the nest for such a short period of time, orphans should be released, if possible, on a pond where there are other broods of the same species of similar age.

If no suitable foster nests can be located, the young should be taken to a wildlife rehabilitation centre (listed on page 76). Do not attempt to hand raise them. While in transport to a rehab. centre, orphaned birds need to be kept warm and should be fed an emergency ration every 20 minutes. If they appear to be cold and lifeless, warm them up by holding them in your hand or against your skin before transferring them to a warm, dark location—a shoebox lined with tissue paper is ideal.

EMERGENCY FOOD

Maggots, mealworms, earthworm pieces, Science Diet Feline Maintenance® (soaked briefly in water or Gatorade®) or the following emergency ration can be administered with a toothpick or tweezers: *Mash two hard-boiled eggs (including shells). Put them in a blender, then add two chopped raw carrots and enough water to make the mixture into a pudding consistency. Add a handful of raisins, a handful of wheat germ and (optional) a handful of chopped fruit. If it is available, add two drops of cage bird vitamin supplement.*

COMPETITORS AND PREDATORS

Thankfully, nestbox trails on the Canadian prairies are not afflicted with the snake or fire ant problems that plague trails in many parts of North America. Like our southern and eastern colleagues, however, we too must deal with several troublesome competitors and predators. Fortunately, predation can usually be minimized through nestbox design and placement, and by using deterrents.

AVIAN COMPETITORS AND PREDATORS

BLUEBIRDS – there have been documented cases, albeit rare, of bluebirds forcibly taking over a nestbox being used by smaller species. To accommodate both, put up another box for the bluebirds close by and exclude them from the already-occupied box by placing hole resticters measuring 25 mm (1 in.) or 29 mm (1 1/8 in.) over the entrance hole.

COWBIRDS – commonly lay their eggs in the nests of other songbirds, and have been known to parasitize nests in nestboxes. The extent of this behavior on the prairies is poorly documented, so Ellis Bird Farm Ltd. would appreciate receiving any records of cowbird parasitism in nestboxes.

EUROPEAN STARLINGS – see page 65.

HOUSE SPARROWS – see page 66.

HAWKS AND OWLS – will dine on both primary and secondary cavity nesters, though they are not usually a problem around nestboxes. Great Horned Owls will quite often prey upon Northern Saw-whet Owls, and they have been known to extract young Purple Martins from their nests. Kestrels have been observed plucking young birds out of nestboxes, and both Red-tailed and Swainson's Hawks have been seen snatching young bluebirds as they make their maiden flight out of the nestbox. There are few measures that can be taken to prevent hawk or owl predation, other than ensuring the nests are deep enough to protect the young. Setting out boxes a safe distance away from known hawk or owl nesting areas may also reduce predation. See the Purple Martin section (pages 44-48) for predator-proofing Purple Martin houses.

MAGPIES AND CROWS – can sometimes be serious predators. They usually sit on the roof of the box and pluck the young out as they come up begging for food. Magpies have also been observed clinging to the front of a nestbox, balancing on the latch of a front-opening style box. The most effective magpie and crow deterrent is to ensure that the box lids are large enough to prevent these crafty predators from being able to reach down to the hole. A smooth front will prevent them from clinging on to the box. If magpies or crows become a problem during the middle of a breeding season, and it is not possible to replace boxes, the roofs and front panels can be retrofitted with large pieces of thin metal or aluminum (offset press plates, available at some newspaper offices, work well).

TREE SWALLOWS - will often compete with bluebirds for nestboxes. Setting boxes out in tandem (6 m to 8 m [20 -25 ft.]) will allow both species to nest peacefully side by side.

WRENS – will sometimes destroy the eggs and young of other birds, including other wrens. Wren competition can usually be minimized by putting wren boxes next to brushy areas, and boxes for other species at least 30 m (100 ft.) from trees.

MAMMALIAN PREDATORS AND PESTS

Mammalian predators can be very serious problems on a nestbox trail. Deterrents are explained in the next section and illustrated on page 17.

BLACK BEARS – will sometimes climb trees or posts and destroy nestboxes and their contents. Use deterrents: A,B,C.

CATS – can be serious predators on a nestbox trail, and are a great menace near human occupation. Use deterrents: A, B, C, D, E, F.

MICE – usually pose a problem because they take up occupancy early in the winter and may occasionally prevent a pair of birds from becoming established the following spring. Their urine also fouls the inside of the box and they will occasionally go into a box and eat the nestlings. Deer Mice will not usually return to the box if evicted, so removing them in mid- or late March will ensure that the box is ready for its intended occupants. Use deterrents: A, B, C, D.

PORCUPINES – can cause problems on nestbox trails through their habit of enlarging the entrance holes or by chewing on the boxes. Use deterrents: A, B, C, D, E, G.

RACCOONS – are common across the southern half of Manitoba and Saskatchewan. Although still rare in Alberta, their population appears to be increasing, especially in the southern part of the province. Raccoon predation is most likely to occur near water, early in the spring, or in drought years when the raccoons' aquatic fare is lacking. Intelligent and dexterous, raccoons are able to make short work of a nestbox and its occupants. Use deterrents: A, B, C, D, E, F.

SQUIRRELS – will readily nest in boxes, and both Red and Flying Squirrels will prey on eggs, young and adult birds. Red Squirrels make larger nests and tend to be more persistent competitors. Flying squirrels will usually abandon the box after being disturbed once. Competition from squirrels can best be avoided by keeping boxes well away from squirrel habitat. Fir plywood at least 19 mm (3/4 in.) thick seems to be too difficult for them to chew through, so should be used in problem areas. Use deterrents: B, C, D, G.

WEASELS – problems are usually localized and occur after a weasel has discovered that it can obtain a free meal in a nestbox. Once it makes this discovery, it may travel from box to box along fences (they can actually run along barbed wire) or trails left by humans, dining on the nestbox occupants. If a weasel becomes a problem, contact a Fish and Wildlife (AB), Conservation (SK) or Department of Natural Resources (DNR) (MB) Officer regarding a damage permit to remove it. Use deterrents: A, B, C, D.

DETERRING CLIMBING PREDATORS

A. Place boxes on a 1.8-m (6-ft.) high pole of very smooth 25-mm (1-in.) metal pipe or 38-mm (1 1/2-in.) PVC.

B. Use conical-shaped baffles below the box. Baffles can be constructed out of sheet metal, printing press plates, from a disk blade, or from a large plastic bucket with the lip removed and secured upside-down beneath the nestbox. Baffles should be at least 61 cm (24 in.) in diameter and placed at least 1.5 m (5 ft.) above the ground. The central hole of disk blades must be enlarged to accommodate the pole. The blades can be supported underneath with clamps, which allow them to tilt freely.

C. Place a piece of stovepipe over the post, or wrap the tree or fencepost with aluminum sheeting (offset press plates, available at some newspaper offices, work well).

D. Apply a heavy coat (19 mm [3/4 in.]) of chassis or white lithium grease over the entire length of post. Chassis grease can be softened by adding a little turpentine.

E. Use entrance hole guards to make it difficult for predators to reach into the box. The simplest is constructed out of a small block of wood with a hole through it and fastened over the entrance hole. Extensive experience with nest box guards by trail operators in the midwestern USA has shown that bluebirds usually avoid a box with an entrance hole thickness of more than 38 mm (1 1/2 in.) total if a thinner entrance is available.

An entrance hole guard that has proven to be very successful and is becoming very popular is the 9 cm x 14 cm (3 1/2 x 5 1/2 in.) rectangular wire mesh guard designed by Jim Noel of Illinois (**E-i**). If this guard is used in pastured areas, the top and bottom of the guard can be made out of wood to prevent the guard from totally collapsing should it be rubbed by cattle (**E-ii**). Don Hutchings of Texas has designed a similar guard from a 10-cm (4-in.) section of 10-cm (4-in.) diameter PVC pipe. The PVC pipe is mounted on a piece of plywood into which a 10-cm (4-in.) hole has been drilled. The apparatus is then fastened onto the front of the nestbox (**E-iii**).

F. Use large roofs to make it difficult for predators to reach down into the entrance hole.

G. Tack a 15-cm^2 (2 1/2-in.^{2}) piece of tin or plastic laminate protector plate around the entrance area (small boxes only) to prevent predators from chewing around the entrance hole.

Examples of predator deterrents

PARASITES AND INSECT PESTS

Thanks to our long cold winters, nestboxes across the prairies attract relatively few parasites. The most serious parasite is the blowfly (order Diptera), whose larvae attach themselves to the nestlings' feet, legs, abdomen, bill, or wing and tail feather shafts and suck their blood. They usually feed at night, then drop to the bottom of the nest during the day. While blowflies rarely kill the nestlings, severe infestations may weaken them, making them vulnerable to malnutrition or hypothermia.

When found attached to a nestling, blowfly larvae should be removed. If some are found in the nesting material, the nest should be lifted and shaken gently to dislodge them. If infestations are severe or if the nest is wet and soggy, replace the nesting material with dry grass.

Insecticides that have pyrethrin, a "natural" insecticide, as the active ingredient, can also be used. Pyrethrin analogs (allethrin, resmethrin, permethrin and tetramethrin) are also acceptable. Make sure these ingredients are not combined with harmful or unproven products. Avoid using other toxic chemicals.

Some trail operators have had success reducing blowflies by placing a hardware cloth platform underneath the nest just before the young are scheduled to hatch. When the larvae drop down through the mesh, they are unable to crawl back up into the nest.

Researchers in Ontario have recently suggested that leaving nesting material in boxes over winter may actually help reduce blowfly problems. They point out that one of the most effective biological control agents of blowflies is a small parasitic wasp, Nasonia. The larvae of these jewel wasps overwinter inside blowfly puparium, then resume development the following spring. Nests that are left inside the box over winter will help increase the population of these allies and will enable them to start their assault against blowflies early in the spring. An alternative to leaving the nests in the box would be to collect and put them in a large pail covered with 3-mm (1/8-in.) screen. The pail should be kept in an outbuilding or other protected place for the winter. When hatching occurs the following spring, the screen will prevent the larger adult blowflies from escaping, but will permit the smaller wasps to exit.

Wasps and bumblebees sometimes take up residence in an empty nestbox or, on occasion, may take over an occupied one. Providing they do not pose a hazard to the trail monitors, it is advisable to just leave them alone. If they need to be destroyed in a box not occupied by birds, spray a pyrethrin-based insecticide into the hole at night, then plug the hole until morning. Grease, petroleum jelly or soft soap can be applied on the inside upper surface of the box to prevent wasps or bumblebees from becoming established.

Lice, fleas, ticks and mites are often found on birds, but are not thought to pose a serious problem unless infestations are very severe.

Ants will sometimes attack nestlings if the nestbox post is placed close to an anthill, or on an ant-infested tree. The best way to remedy an ant problem is to simply move the box to a more appropriate location. Applying a thick layer of grease beneath the box or placing grease-covered wooden spools between the box and the post will exclude them. They may also be discouraged from using a nestbox if a pinch of tobacco or a few coffee grounds are placed on the floor.

LYME DISEASE

Lyme disease is a debilitating disease of humans, wildlife and domestic animals. The first North American outbreak of the disease in humans occurred in Lyme, Connecticut in 1975. Although it is not a serious health concern on the Canadian prairies, nestbox trail operators should be aware of it.

Lyme disease has reached epidemic proportions in California and the northern USA. In Alberta, it may occur in the foothills, mountains and aspen parkland areas, although the ticks responsible for transmitting the disease, *Ixodes dammini* and *I. pacificus,* have not been reported in the province and there have been no confirmed cases of transmission within Alberta. There have been two reported cases of Lyme disease in Saskatchewan as of March 1992, though it is suspected that both cases were contracted outside that province. Two adult *I. dammini* have been positively identified in Manitoba, but it is likely that these specimens originated elsewhere, and were transported by birds. There are no known areas of Manitoba where the tick is endemic.

Lyme disease is acquired when an individual is bitten by a tick infected with the bacterium, *Borrelia burgdorferi*. A wide variety of wild vertebrates, principally small mammals and ground-frequenting birds, may carry *B. burgdorferi* in their blood, and ticks transmit infection from host-to-host. Biting flies may also carry the bacterium.

These ticks use three hosts, feeding on a new animal at each of the three stages of their life cycle. Although most commonly associated with White-footed and Deer Mice, the larvae and nymphs of the ticks have been recorded from 29 species of mammals and from 49 species of birds, most of which live on or near the ground. The adult ticks, which have a narrower host range, have not been reported from birds. A tick that is embedded and engorged in a bird's skin will not let go to attach itself to the person handling the bird, but there is a slim chance that an unattached tick may move to the person holding the bird.

Bites from most ticks are virtually painless, so they may not be noticed immediately. Since the transmission of *B. burgdorferi* does not happen for the first 12-24 hours after attaching, removal of the tick as soon as possible is likely to reduce the risk of acquiring the disease. If found, the tick should be grasped by the base of its mouthparts with fine-bladed tweezers or a special tick-removal device, at the level of the skin, and pulled straight out to ensure that no mouthparts are left in the skin. Do not attempt to pull it out by grabbing its body and squeezing since this may inject the Lyme bacteria into the wound. Do not try to remove it using matches, cigarettes or petroleum jelly.

The bite site should be cleansed with disinfectant, and hands should be washed after removing the tick. The tick should be taken to a doctor so that it can be tested for the bacteria.

Lyme disease can be debilitating and chronic, so early diagnosis is important. The disease can be avoided with treatment if caught in the early stages. Persons developing a flu-like illness, especially if accompanied by a spreading red rash, 3-5 days following an insect/tick bite, or frequenting an area where Lyme disease is known to occur, should see their doctor and refer to their history of possible exposure.

People who spend a lot of time outdoors are at the greatest risk of exposure, since they can pick up an infected tick when they walk through brush and tall grass in midsummer when tick nymphs are most active. Precautions against infection include: wearing light-coloured long-sleeve shirts and long pants (pants should be tucked into socks); applying insect repellents to clothing; removing any ticks from clothing before they reach the skin; searching for ticks on the body after outdoor activity; and removing any attached ticks as soon as possible.

Effective tick repellents include Permanone®, Perma-Kill® and Duranon®. A new outerwear garment, Tick Chaps®, which can be worn over pants or shorts, is now available in the USA. These chaps have elastic bands at the bottom and a loose pleat around the thigh which acts as a barrier to the ticks in their upward climb. An absorbent strip of material is sewn to a nonabsorbent backing beneath the tick flap which can be sprayed with tick repellent. For more information contact Forest Mate, Box 600, Antigo, WI 54409.

For more information on Lyme disease, contact a local health clinic in Alberta or Saskatchewan. In Manitoba, contact Manitoba Health, Communicable Disease Control (Winnipeg) or the Manitoba Department of Natural Resources. A book on Lyme disease is available from Dr. Jo Ann Heltzel, 3714 York Circle, Woodbury, MN 55125. Lyme prevention products are available from SCS Ltd., Box 573, Stony Pt., NY 10980. Phone: (914) 429-5394.

CAVITY-NESTING BIRDS OF THE PRAIRIES

There are at least 42 species of cavity-nesting birds that breed on the Canadian prairies. We have listed them here in taxonomic order (the order in field guides), and have included both primary and secondary cavity nesters. Some species descriptions are more detailed than others. In most cases, this reflects the "popularity" of a species or the degree to which it has been researched. Egg numbers given indicate average clutch sizes, with extremes shown in brackets. Nestbox plans for the larger cavity nesters are shown on pages 35-36 while those for the smaller ones are shown on pages 72-73.

There are some species that, although not classified as cavity nesters, will sometimes take up residency in a nestbox. Such species include the Common Grackle *(Quiscalus quiscula)*, Black-billed Magpie *(Pica pica)* and Eastern Kingbird *(Tyrannus tyrannus)*. Ellis Bird Farm Ltd. would be interested in hearing from anyone who has had these, or any other, unusual species use their nestboxes.

DUCKS

Ducks belong to a worldwide family, Anatidae, which are aquatic, web-footed birds that spend most of their time in or around water. Nestbox plans for ducks are shown on pages 35-36.

CAVITY-NESTING DUCKS

Extensive research on cavity-nesting ducks has shown that nestboxes can play a major role in restoring nesting habitat and establishing new breeding populations in species such as Wood Duck, Common Goldeneye and Barrow's Goldeneye. In areas where the Bufflehead population may be limited by nest sites, such as in the boreal forest areas dominated by conifers, the addition of suitable nestboxes may increase breeding density. Nestboxes may help to increase clutch size, and, if properly constructed, erected and protected with predator guards, may ensure greater hatching success, since they are not as vulnerable to predation or natural deterioration as are natural cavities.

Some male and female ducks pair-bond in the fall, while others pick their mates on the wintering grounds or during migration. With the exception of the Wood Duck, female cavity-nesting ducks do not breed until they are at least 2 years old. When they arrive on the breeding grounds, females fly through the woods prospecting for potential nest cavities. Shortly after the nesting season, usually during June and early July, yearling females will go into nest cavities, apparently investigating them for use the following year.

Cavity-nesting ducks tend to defend either a defined territory on the water or a mobile territory around the female while she is on the water. This is in contrast to the other cavity nesters, which defend their nest site and the area around it. Because of this habit, nestboxes for ducks can be placed very close together. Ducks do not bring nesting material into the nest, so shavings or straw, which protect and insulate the eggs, should be placed in the boxes before the nesting season.

As egg laying progresses, the female plucks the down from her breast area to expose a brood patch. She presses this area of warm skin against the eggs to keep them warm. The down is used to line her nest and to cover the eggs when she leaves to feed. Unlike all other cavity nesters, whose young are hatched naked and helpless, ducklings are ready to leave the nest only 24 to 36 hours after hatching. They use their sharp claws to climb to the opening of the box, then tumble to the ground in response to the calls by the female as she waits on the ground or water below. The young never return to the nest cavity after fledging. Duckling mortality is very high; it is estimated that only 50 percent of the young reach the flight stage.

Female ducks sometimes practise nest parasitism, which is the habit of a hen laying an egg in the nest of another female. The eggs are then incubated by the foster mother along with her own clutch. Sometimes, however, the parasitized female will abandon her nest. Several hens will sometimes lay their eggs in the same nest. These nests, called dump nests, may contain up to 30 eggs and can be easily identified because usually no attempt is made to cover the eggs nor to incubate them.

If hens of different species attempt to use the same nestbox, mixed clutches will occur. In some cases, all the eggs hatch and a female will then care for her own offspring as well as those of a different species!

Females that nest successfully will tend to return to the same breeding grounds or even the same nestbox year after year, while those that experience a nest failure often select a new site. You should not be discouraged if your duck boxes remain unused the year you put them out. It may take a season or two for females to find them, then it will take another two years before the daughters, which generally return to their natal area, are of breeding age. Once you get ducks established in your boxes, you will find that nestbox occupancy, especially after the third year, will gradually increase.

WOOD DUCK

(Aix sponsa)

Eggs: 8-10 *(nest parasitism may affect clutch size)*
Incubation Period: 27-33 days
Time in Nest: 24-36 hours

The male Wood Duck has a crown and crest of iridescent green and purple, and a face of purple with two white markings extending up from a white throat. The adult female has a short crest and a large, white, teardrop-shaped eye patch. The bill of both sexes angles downward and both have long, squared-off tails. They have sharp claws and sometimes perch on snags, stumps, branches or on top of buildings.

The Wood Duck's diet consists of aquatic plants supplemented with insects.

DISTRIBUTION

Alberta – local and uncommon, but their range appears to be expanding. Occasionally reported during spring migration. Since they are commonly raised in zoos, some sightings may be of escapees. Most confirmed nesting records are from the Medicine Hat area. Several have been released in Calgary, and the population in that area is increasing.

Saskatchewan – common on the Souris River downstream from Estevan. Found breeding in small numbers along the Qu'Appelle River and in the Duck Mountain, Hudson Bay and Cumberland House regions. Rare elsewhere in the province.

Manitoba – uncommon, but breed across most of the southern part of the province. Breed along the Assiniboine and Seine rivers and in Whiteshell Provincial Park. In the southwestern part of the province, they frequent the Antler, Souris, Little Saskatchewan and Pembina rivers and associated backwaters. They breed in Turtle Mountain Provincial Park and in the area around and including Spruce Woods Provincial Heritage Park.

NESTING

Wood Ducks court and pair during the fall and winter. They arrive on their breeding grounds soon after the ice has melted, usually in early to mid-April. In Manitoba, they have initiated egg laying as early as the second week in April.

Nest cavities are not always located near water. Before the nesting period, the drakes defend only a small, mobile territory around the hen. They remain with their mates longer than most ducks, usually until the eggs are pipped. Wood Duck eggs are buffy white, and clutch sizes vary widely as a result of predation and nest parasitism.

Unlike other cavity-nesting ducks, most female Wood Ducks breed as yearlings. The young are able to fly about 63 days after hatching.

NESTBOXES

Wood Duck boxes should be located close to quiet wooded streams, backwaters or beaver ponds that have overhanging vegetation rooted on gently sloping banks.

The traditional recommendation for Wood Duck box placement has been to erect several boxes close together in a highly visible area, such as over open water. Recent research, however, has revealed that these locations are less than ideal because densely clumped, highly visible boxes tend to suffer high rates of nest dumping. Some researchers suggest that nestbox productivity is maximized if boxes are placed at low densities and in locations that mimic natural cavities and are less visible.

Raccoons, which are not yet a major problem on the prairies, are the most serious predator of Wood Ducks in other parts of their range. In Manitoba, Gray and Red Squirrels are thought to be the most serious detriment to breeding populations since they remove eggs, fill the nest cavities with leaves and twigs, and build their nests over active bird nests.

Ellis Bird Farm Ltd. would be interested in receiving reports of Wood Ducks using nestboxes in Alberta.

BARROW'S GOLDENEYE

(Bucephala islandica)

Eggs: 8-14 (nest parasitism may affect clutch size)
Incubation Period: 30 days
Time in Nest: 24-36 hours

The male Barrow's Goldeneye has a white crescent on each side of its purplish-black face. The dark color of the back extends forward in a bar which partially separates the white breast from the white sides. The female and eclipse-plumaged males closely resemble female Common Goldeneyes. The head shape of the Barrow's (puffy, oval-shaped, steep forehead) separates it from the Common (peaked with a sloping forehead). The bright orange bill of the female Barrow's in winter and spring turns dark brown during incubation. The orange color returns sometime in the fall. Both sexes have yellow eyes.

Barrow's Goldeneyes feed on insects, roots and aquatic weeds.

DISTRIBUTION

Alberta – breed in the foothills and Rocky Mountains. In spite of a lack of confirmed nesting records, numerous sightings suggest summer residence, and probable breeding, in the northern areas of the province.

Saskatchewan – no breeding records.

Manitoba – no breeding records.

NESTING

Barrow's Goldeneyes arrive during the early stages of spring breakup. While old Pileated Woodpecker cavities are the sites most often used, they have also been known to lay their dull greenish eggs in crow nests, marmot burrows, ground cavities and holes in cliffs. Flicker holes that have been enlarged by decay are also used.

Both sexes of Barrow's Goldeneye are very territorial. Paired males defend territories on wintering areas, and in the spring they defend territories on breeding ponds against all other ducks. The defence of these territories, which are established along the shoreline, and which are maintained even when the female is absent, allows her to feed undisturbed.

Females with broods are also territorially aggressive. Studies have shown that they exclude all adult goldeneyes from their territories, are aggressive toward other species and even attack and kill ducklings of other species. Female aggression may also limit goldeneye brood density on small lakes and increases Bufflehead duckling mortality in some areas.

When incubation is half completed, the males leave their mates and flock with other males and undergo the molt. Females molt later than the males, and in different areas. By mid-July, most females abandon their broods and congregate with other females on large lakes. Their molt is usually complete by early September, though it is believed that they remain on their molting lakes until ice formation. Barrow's Goldeneyes generally winter along the Pacific coast.

NESTBOXES

Nestboxes for Barrow's Goldeneyes should be placed near large lakes or along rivers.

COMMON GOLDENEYE

(Bucephala clangula)

Eggs: 6-14 (nest parasitism may affect clutch size)
Incubation Period: 27-32 days
Time in Nest: 24-36 hours

The Common Goldeneye is often referred to by its nickname "Whistler" because of the whistling noise made by its rapidly beating wings. The male has a greenish head (which often appears black) with a white spot on each side of the face. The bill of the Common Goldeneye is long and less sloping than that of the Barrow's. The female, which closely resembles the female Barrow's Goldeneye, has a brown head. From mid-fall to spring, the bill of the female is dark with a yellowish tip. At the onset of incubation, this color disappears and the beak remains brown until the yellowish color is regained sometime in the fall. Both sexes have yellow eyes.

Common Goldeneyes feed on aquatic plants and insects.

DISTRIBUTION

Alberta – breed throughout the northern and central parts of the province (south to Calgary) and in the Cypress Hills.

Saskatchewan – found throughout the province's parkland, mixed-wood and boreal forest regions and Cypress Hills.

Manitoba – found throughout most of the province. In the southeast, they breed along the Red River and at Lake Winnipeg. They are also common nesters at Island Park at Portage La Prairie and in Riding Mountain National Park.

NESTING

The Common Goldeneye is one of the first duck species to return to the prairies in the spring. Drakes defend a specific territory on the water, not just the area around the female and not always near the nest site. The male will sometimes accompany the female to the nest early in the season, but usually remains on his territory and defends it while waiting for the return of his mate. The male remains on-territory until mid- or even late incubation, at which time he leaves to join other drakes as they undergo their molt. Common Goldeneyes tend to be somewhat less aggressive than Barrow's Goldeneyes, but, like the Barrow's, exclude all other goldeneyes and Buffleheads from their territory.

A clutch of greenish eggs is laid at a rate of about one egg per day.

Competition for nest sites sometimes occurs between Buffleheads and goldeneyes. Buffleheads, which are smaller, are usually out-competed for boxes with large entrance holes. Mixed clutches and mixed broods of goldeneyes/mergansers and goldeneyes/Buffleheads sometimes occur.

The young are able to fly at about 8 weeks of age.

Goldeneyes spend the fall on staging lakes and then migrate to their coastal wintering areas during lake freeze-up. Some Common Goldeneyes overwinter throughout the prairies in open water areas.

NESTBOXES

Nestboxes for Common Goldeneyes should be placed near wooded ponds and lakes or along rivers.

BUFFLEHEAD

(Bucephala albeola)

Eggs: 8-12 (nest parasitism may affect clutch size)
Incubation Period: 29 days
Time in Nest: 24-36 hours

The Bufflehead is the smallest of our cavity-nesting ducks. The male is distinguished by a puffy black and white head. The female is a duller gray-black with a small, elongated white patch on each side of her head.

Buffleheads eat invertebrates, aquatic insects and snails. Seeds of water plants are eaten in some areas.

DISTRIBUTION

Alberta – breed in the central and northern forested regions, less commonly in the foothills and Rocky Mountains.

Saskatchewan – breed throughout the parkland, mixed-wood and boreal forest areas.

Manitoba – uncommon breeders throughout most of the province, especially in the parkland area.

NESTING

Buffleheads pair-bond during or before spring migration. They arrive on the southern prairies in early April and nest from early May until early July.

Buffleheads rely almost exclusively on old flicker holes for nesting sites, so the retention of aspen forests adjacent to lakes and ponds is essential for the survival of this species.

The male usually leaves the area during the middle or late stages of incubation to join other drakes and yearlings on nearby lakes and ponds.

Bufflehead eggs are creamy white. The young stay with their mother for approximately six weeks, when she then abandons them to head to molting lakes. The young are able to fly at 50-55 days of age. In the fall, Buffleheads will gather in open water of large lakes, and may remain until November. A few occasionally overwinter on prairie rivers that have open water.

NESTBOXES

Buffleheads prefer to nest around small, wooded lakes and ponds, not along rivers or near large lakes.

Unlike goldeneyes, female Buffleheads are not easily flushed from their nests. Where both species occur, there is often competition for nesting sites and the goldeneyes will usually out-compete the Buffleheads for larger boxes. If you have both species in your area, you should put out the appropriate-sized boxes to accommodate both species.

COMMON MERGANSER

(Mergus merganser)

Eggs: 7-14 (15)
Incubation Period: 28-32 days
Time in Nest: 24-36 hours

These large ducks, called Goosanders in Europe, have long, slim necks and thin, hooked red bills. The male has a green head and white breast while the female has a bright chestnut, crested head, white chin and white breast.

Fish form a substantial part of their diet.

DISTRIBUTION

Alberta – breed in the Rocky Mountains, foothills, northern boreal forest and in the northwest sections of the parkland.

Saskatchewan – breed in the mixed-wood and boreal forest areas as well as along the South Saskatchewan River and in the Cypress Hills. Uncommon and local in the parkland and prairies.

Manitoba – common throughout most of the northern, southeastern and a small portion of southwestern regions.

NESTING

Common Mergansers will nest in hollow trees, on the ground, on cliff ledges and in nestboxes.

Their eggs are a pale buff colour and are laid at intervals of more than one day. The male leaves the breeding area early in the incubation stage. Several broods may join together after fledging, forming aggregations of 20 or more.

Young mergansers attain first flight at about 65 days, with some probably taking 70 days or more. Late-hatched young do not fly until mid-September. Because it takes the young so long to reach the flight stage, late-hatched broods may suffer losses when water areas freeze prematurely.

Common Mergansers overwinter in open water near Calgary and Banff in Alberta, at Squaw Rapids and Gardiner Dam in Saskatchewan, and a few other isolated locations. It is not known if or where they overwinter in Manitoba.

NESTBOXES

Common Mergansers prefer to nest near the shores of rivers and lakes, and require clear water with sufficient fish of proper size for the ducklings. Although the use of nestboxes by this species is not frequently reported, they would no doubt use more boxes if they were provided in suitable habitat.

HOODED MERGANSER

(Lophodytes cucullatus)

Eggs: 5-12
Incubation Period: 31 days
Time in Nest: 24-36 hours

The Hooded Merganser is the smallest of the mergansers but has the largest crest. The pattern of the black and white crest on the male is distinctive. The female is brownish overall with a dark head and crest, and dark upper and yellowish lower mandibles.

Hooded Mergansers eat fish, crustaceans, aquatic insects, frogs, tadpoles and aquatic plants.

DISTRIBUTION

Alberta – the only confirmed nesting records are from the Rocky Mountain regions, though it is thought that the species breeds sparingly throughout the northern forest region of the province.

Saskatchewan – breeding distribution is poorly known, nesting records are scattered across the eastern mixed-wood and parkland forest areas. Large fall concentrations suggest a larger breeding population than nest records indicate. Some non-breeding birds are seen on water bodies in the grasslands during July and August.

Manitoba – uncommon breeders in the southern and central parts of the province. In the southeast, they nest regularly in Whiteshell Provincial Park, and in southwest are local nesters in Turtle Mountain Provincial Park, Spruce Woods Provincial Heritage Park and Riding Mountain National Park. They are also found along the Little Saskatchewan and Pembina river valleys.

NESTING

Hooded Mergansers arrive on the prairies between early April and early May, often in association with Common and Red-breasted Mergansers. They nest in tree cavities, hollow logs, holes in banks or nestboxes.

They lay white, almost-round eggs. The young fly at about 71 days of age.

Hooded Mergansers feed in ponds and quiet clear waters, but will move to swift-flowing streams when other areas are frozen. Drainage of wetlands and the destruction of forests that contain suitable nesting sites have had an impact on the population of this species.

NESTBOXES

Very little is known about nestbox use by Hooded Mergansers. Boxes for them can be set out around ponds, rivers and sheltered backwaters. They are not likely to use boxes set near large lakes.

Ellis Bird Farm Ltd. would be interested in receiving any records of Hooded Mergansers using nestboxes.

SETTING OUT DUCK BOXES

NESTBOX DESIGN

We highly recommend the nestbox designed by Jim Potter and Jim Allen of Red Deer, AB. See pages 35-36 for design and construction details.

SITE SELECTION AND BOX PLACEMENT

While habitat preferences vary among species, all sites must be close to a permanent water body. Permanent water is essential for duckling survival since they are very vulnerable to predation until they are old enough to fly. Potholes and sloughs that dry up in the early summer should not be used. Campgrounds, fishing paths and other areas with frequent human disturbance should also be avoided. Some good sites are easier to access after ponds and streams are frozen.

The trek to water is very hazardous for young ducks, so boxes should be placed as close as possible to the water's edge and in areas where underbrush is minimal. The entrance hole should face towards the water, away from prevailing winds. A clear flight path should be visible from the water.

Boxes should be attached with lag bolts or spikes to large, live trees. If bolts are used, they should be loosened periodically to allow for tree growth. Make sure the box tilts slightly forward so the ducklings can climb out. The tilt will also assist in keeping rain and snow from blowing into the entrance hole. Avoid dead trees, which are prone to blow-down, and young aspens, which are often cut down by beaver. If beaver are active in the area, loosely wrap the bottom 1 m (3 ft.) of the tree with stucco wire (allow room for tree growth). Make sure the wire is secured by a staple or nail, and make sure it is set firmly on the ground around the entire tree.

To maximize use of boxes, place a Bufflehead box directly above a goldeneye box on the same tree. This provides nesting space for both species.

Starlings may try to nest in the smaller box, and since they are somewhat territorial, they will prevent another pair of starlings from occupying the larger goldeneye box. Nestbox use by starlings tends to decrease in direct proportion to increased goldeneye use, so most paired boxes will eventually be used only by Buffleheads and goldeneyes. In addition to competing for nest sites, starlings may also cause nest desertion by covering the eggs with nesting material. To discourage starling use, cover the entrance hole or plug it with a stick in the fall and remove it in late April (earlier if ducks are seen in the vicinity). Starlings are usually laying by this time, so most will have located another nesting cavity. If a starling nest is found (blue eggs), it should be removed.

If Red Squirrels use a duck box, their nesting material will often fill the box and should be removed. The smaller Flying Squirrel nests can be left, since the ducks will nest on top of this material.

If predation becomes a problem, move the box to a metal pole or to a lone tree that cannot be reached from adjacent trees. Predator guards can also be used.

MONITORING

Duck boxes should be inspected periodically to determine use, maintenance requirements and predation. Ducks are very sensitive to disturbance, so boxes should be inspected only once or twice after egg laying has commenced. Since most hens lay their eggs in the morning, disturbance will be reduced if boxes are monitored only in the afternoon. Tufts of down around the entrance hole are a sure sign that incubation is taking place.

If you do not plan to monitor your duck boxes regularly, especially in the early spring, set out the larger goldeneye or merganser boxes. These boxes tend to be used by a greater variety of species and seem to be less attractive to European Starlings.

To monitor a box during the nesting season, approach it from the rear while making a bit of noise (e.g., heavy walking). Tap or scratch lightly on the tree or pole below the box. If nothing happens, check the box quietly. If the hen can be heard scrambling to the entrance hole, remain quiet until she takes flight or returns to the eggs. If she leaves, the nest can be inspected. If she returns to her eggs, leave her alone and walk quietly away from the box.

Boxes can also be checked during the winter for nesting success and maintenance requirements. At this time, egg fragments, addled eggs and nesting debris can be removed and clean shavings added. Nest success can be determined by the presence of egg sac membranes and bits of eggshell in the bottom of the box. You will also be able to determine, by the color of the eggshells, which species used the box.

Monitoring a duck box

Kestrels belong to the family Falconidae, which includes birds of prey noted for their notched beaks, short necks, long pointed wings, short to medium-long tapered tails, and relatively large feet. They have extraordinary eyesight and some species can dive at incredible speeds. Nestbox plans for kestrels are shown on pages 35-36.

AMERICAN KESTREL

(Falco sparverius)

Eggs: 3-5 (2-7)
Incubation Period: 28-32 days
Time in Nest: 25-31 days

American Kestrels, once called "Sparrow Hawks", are North America's smallest falcons. They can be easily identified by their small size, reddish color on the back and tail, and bold, black facial markings. Males and females show a marked difference in plumage; the female has brown wings while the male's are blue.

Kestrels are considered to be very beneficial birds to humans because their main prey species are rodents and insects (especially grasshoppers). They will also prey on the occasional small bird, so boxes should be set up at least 1 km (0.6 mi.) from a bluebird trail or Purple Martin colony.

It should be noted that kestrels, like all species at the upper levels of the food chain, may be adversely affected by the use of rodenticides and insecticides on their prey species.

DISTRIBUTION

Kestrels are widely distributed throughout the three provinces, except in the extreme northern sections.

NESTING

Kestrels usually arrive back from their wintering grounds in the south during early to mid-April and are our most common small hawk in summer. They are often seen perched on tall dead trees or utility lines, or hovering above roadside ditches in search of prey.

When the male arrives on the breeding territory, he localizes his activities to a territory that includes several hunting areas and potential nest sites. For nesting sites, kestrels will use cavities in trees, nestboxes, cliff crevices, old magpie nests, bank burrows or recesses in buildings. Although the female may explore nest sites on her own, the male seems to induce her to follow him to a favored cavity within his territory.

Once pair-bonded, the male remains on the hunting ground where he catches prey for himself and his mate. The female usually remains in the vicinity of the nest, where she spends her time resting, preening, incubating eggs or feeding on the prey brought to her by her mate. The habit of courtship-feeding actually starts while the female is still capable of hunting for herself—long before she is laying eggs or incubating.

When a nest site is chosen, the female lays her white, creamy or pale pink, brownish-spotted eggs at two- to three- day intervals. No nesting material is brought into the nest. Incubation commences before the last egg is laid and is done primarily by the female, although the male does assist. Hatching takes place over a period of three to four days and the young are brooded continuously for the first few days. When the young are 1.5 to 2 weeks old, the female begins to assist the male in finding food for their hungry brood.

Kestrel nestlings have a unique method of disposing of their waste material—they lift up their tails and squirt it onto the walls of the box! By the time the young are ready to leave the nest, the entire inside of the nestbox is coated with a thick layer of feces. The reasons for this behavior are not completely understood. Some researchers suggest that the nestlings may squirt in this fashion to whitewash the nest cavity to reflect sunlight. Whatever the reason, it does minimize the mess on the floor of the cavity.

By the time they are 20 days old, the young are able to feed themselves on the food that the parents bring into the box. Although they fledge at about 1 month of age, they may actually take a few days to completely leave the nest, because they practise flying during the day and then return to the nest at night. The fledglings remain dependent on their parents for food for approximately two weeks. Where kestrels are abundant, large groups of newly independent juveniles may be seen hunting together in late summer. The main fall migrational movements take place during the last week of August and the first two weeks of September, but some of the birds remain until the end of October with a few occasionally overwintering.

NESTBOXES FOR KESTRELS

Kestrels are readily attracted to nestboxes set out in a variety of habitats and locations. Boxes placed adjacent to open fields and meadows or along edges of forests seem to be most attractive. Roadways, clearings and clearcuts that provide hunting areas are also preferred habitats.

Kestrel nestboxes should be placed on a tree or pole and spaced at approximately 1 km (0.6 mi) apart. They should be located where a tall tree, pole or wire is within 100-200 m (330-650 ft.), because they prefer high perches near their nests. The entrance holes should not be hindered by overhanging branches.

Nestboxes do not have to be placed high off the ground. Several kestrel trail operators report success using boxes placed just 1 m (3.3 ft.) above ground level. Predation and disturbance problems will be reduced, however, if the boxes are placed at least 2 m (6-7 ft.) high and protected from predators by a wrap of tin or aluminum below the box. Nestboxes can be set out facing any direction. Recent research indicates that box orientation does not affect nest-box choice nor breeding success.

Approximately 2.5 cm (1 in.) of straw or shavings should be added to the bottom of a kestrel nestbox. This helps keep the eggs warm, reduces the risk of egg damage and keeps the eggs from rolling to the edges of the box. Do not add more than 5 cm (2 in.) of shavings because the eggs are often covered, which reduces the effectiveness of incubation. Kestrel boxes should be checked at the end of the season and cleaned and/or replenished with shavings as required.

European Starlings will compete with kestrels for nestboxes. To prevent starlings from becoming established, monitor the box from a safe distance (preferably with binoculars from about 30 m [100 ft.]) at least weekly during the early part of the breeding season. If kestrels have successfully claimed the box, they will probably be perched somewhere nearby. Once you have established that the female has been incubating at least two weeks, the box can then be monitored on a weekly basis. If starlings take over the box, destroy their nest. If they insist on returning to the box, it should be moved or the entrance hole sealed up.

Kestrels appear to accept human habitation, since they will nest in and around farm or acreage buildings. One style of nestbox that has been successful in attracting them to farmyards was designed by Luke DeWitt and Zoltan Gulyas of Calgary, Alberta. This box, shown below, is attached to the inside of an outside wall of a barn or other building. The box measures 26.7 cm (10 1/2 in.) wide, 30.5 cm (12 in.) deep and 33 cm (13 in.) high. Access to the box is provded by a 7.6-cm (3-in.) entrance hole drilled through the wall of the building.

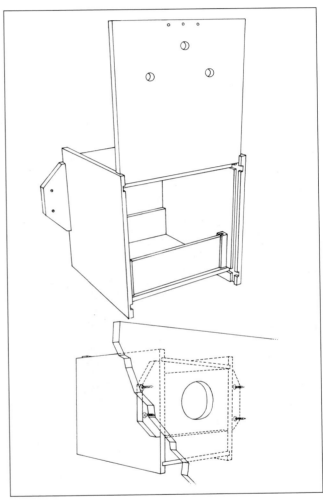

Kestrel nestbox that attaches to the inside of a building

KESTREL KARETAKERS

Kestrel Karetakers, an organization dedicated to the conservation of American Kestrels, was founded in 1975 by Roger Jones of Falls Church, VA, USA.

This informal group encourages the use of nestboxes for kestrels and collects productivity data. An occasional newsletter is published, and membership is by donation.

Contact: Roger Jones, 3549 Devon Drive, Falls Church, VA 22042. Phone: (703) 533-2114.

OWLS

Owls found on the Canadian prairies belong to the family Strigidae, most of which are nocturnal birds of prey renowned for their exceptionally keen sight and hearing. Their physical characteristics include short, strong, hooked bills, large eyes that are directed forward and fixed in the skull, and outer toes that may be moved in either a forward or backward position. Their wings have serrations on the front edge of first primaries which, along with soft body feathers, allow them to fly silently.

OWLS AND NESTBOXES

Cavity-nesting owl species usually use old woodpecker holes or natural cavities for nesting sites. With the exception of Barred, Screech-, Northern Saw-whet and Burrowing Owls, there is very little information about their use of nestboxes. Ellis Bird Farm Ltd. would be very interested in receiving any reports of nestbox use by owls. Nestbox plans for owls are shown on pages 35-36.

BARRED OWL

(Strix varia)
Eggs: *2-3 (4)*
Incubation Period: *28-33 days*
Time in Nest: *5-7 weeks*

Barred Owls are large, chunky brown owls with dark eyes. They have dark barring on the upper breast and dark streaking below. Their calls are often given during the day, and include a distinctive, rhythmic series of loud hoots: *who-cooks-for-you, who-cooks-for-you-all* and a drawn-out *hoo-ah*, sometimes preceded by an ascending agitated barking.

Nocturnal, Barred Owls prey mainly on mice but will take other mammals, small birds and insects.

DISTRIBUTION

Alberta – scarce nester in the central and western parts of the province, where they are resident. Although a rare species in the province, they appear to be increasing in numbers and distribution, especially in the coniferous regions of the upper foothills and Rocky Mountains.

Saskatchewan – uncommon resident across the central mixed-wood forest, becoming rare west of Prince Albert National Park. Locally common near Duck Mountain and Squaw Rapids.

Manitoba – uncommon resident in the south-central, south-eastern and parts of southwestern portions of the province. They prefer coniferous and mixed-wood areas, and are found at Beaudry Provincial Park in the southeast or Spruce Woods Provincial Heritage Park and Riding Mountain National Park in the southwest. Barred Owls sometimes wander during the winter in Manitoba and have occurred at Rivers.

NESTING

Barred Owls nest in tree cavities, in the open end of snags, and old abandoned hawk or crow nests. They typically use the same nest site for many years. Their eggs are white and incubation is performed by the female. Young Barred Owls have the interesting habit of being able to climb up tree trunks using their beaks, talons and wings. This enables them to crawl out of the nest and up to a perch, or to climb back up to the nest should they happen to fall out.

NESTBOXES

The entrance hole on a Barred Owl box should be put into side B so the owlets can use the shaving stop and the top of the hinged side as steps (see pages 35-36).

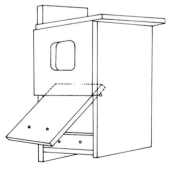

Barred Owl nestbox

Nestboxes for Barred Owls should be set out in late winter. The box should be located 6 m to 9 m (20-30 ft.) high in a mature mixed-wood forest, preferably within 60 m (200 ft.) of water. The box should not be placed at the edge of a clearing nor close to a human residence. The entrance hole should be unobstructed, but a perch near the nestbox should be provided.

EASTERN SCREECH-OWL

(Otus asio)
Eggs: *4-5 (3-7)*
Incubation Period: *27-30 days*
Time in Nest: *6-8 weeks*

Eastern Screech-Owls are the only small owls with ear tufts. They have yellow eyes, feathered toes, heavily streaked upper breasts and either cinnamon (red color phase) or gray (gray color phase) upperparts.

Eastern Screech-Owls seldom *screech;* rather their call is most often a rapidly descending *whinny.* Other calls include trills, yelps and barks.

The diet of Eastern Screech-Owls, which are nocturnal, consists of mice, insects and the occasional bird.

DISTRIBUTION

Alberta – no breeding records.

Saskatchewan – nest irregularly as far west as Moose Jaw, and regularly in the wooded portions of the Souris River, especially downstream from Estevan (Roche Perce). No confirmed records, but it is speculated that they nest annually in the Qu'Appelle and tributary valleys and in the Cypress Hills.

Manitoba – nest along the river bottom woodlands of the Red and Assiniboine rivers. In the southwestern portion of the province, they breed at Lyleton and along the Antler and Little Souris rivers.

NESTING

Eastern Screech-Owls are usually nonmigratory and will usually leave an area only in response to food scarcity. Although they are woodland owls, they will often be attracted to small forested areas. They are quite secretive, so their nests are difficult to find, especially during the breeding season. They do not line their nests, and the white eggs are incubated by the female. They seem to prefer nesting in old Northern Flicker and Pileated Woodpecker cavities.

NESTBOXES

Eastern Screech-Owls will be attracted to nestboxes placed in or at the edge of wooded areas adjacent to fields or wetlands. Nestboxes set out for Wood Ducks are frequently used by these owls for both nesting and roosting.

NORTHERN PYGMY-OWL

(Glaucidium gnoma)

Eggs: *4-6 (3-7)*
Incubation Period: *28 days*
Time in Nest: *29-32 days*

This tiny owl has a long tail that is dark brown with pale bars. Its upperparts are either rusty-brown or gray-brown. Its eyes are actually yellow, but on the back of its neck are black spots that look like eyes. The Northern Pygmy-Owl's call is a mellow, whistled *hoo* or *hoo hoo* repeated in a well-spaced series. It is active during the day, especially in the early mornings and evenings.

Northern Pygmy-Owls are aggressive predators, eating mice, large insects, ground squirrels, chipmunks, pocket gophers and garter snakes. They also prey on songbirds, sometimes catching birds larger than themselves. Songbirds become very agitated when a Northern Pygmy-Owl is close-by and may sometimes be attracted by a person imitating the owl's call.

DISTRIBUTION

Alberta – resident breeder in the Rocky Mountains and foothills.

Saskatchewan – no breeding records.

Manitoba – no breeding records.

NESTING

For nesting, Northern Pygmy-Owls require open stands of coniferous forests or mixed woodlands with an adequate proportion of conifers.

Old Hairy Woodpecker or Northern Flicker holes are usually used. Natural cavities are used less frequently. The nest is usually unlined and the clutch of white or cream-colored eggs is incubated by the female. The nestlings are fed in the nest by both parents.

NESTBOXES

Nestbox use by Northern Pygmy-Owls is not known. Ellis Bird Farm Ltd. would appreciate receiving reports of them using nestboxes.

NORTHERN SAW-WHET OWL

(Aegolius acadicus)
Eggs: *3-6 (10)*
Incubation Period: *21-28 days*
Time in Nest: *28-33 days*

The Northern Saw-whet Owl is a small nocturnal owl similar to the Boreal Owl except for its black beak and streaked forehead. Its breast is reddish-brown above and white below with reddish streaks. Juveniles have very tawny-red breasts and conspicuous white eyebrows. In the breeding season, it roosts during the day in or near its nesting cavity. During the winter, it roosts on the branch of a conifer, usually close to the end of the branch.

The diet of the Northern Saw-whet consists of voles, mice, shrews, insects and the occasional small bird.

DISTRIBUTION

Alberta – breed throughout the southern half of the province west into the Rocky Mountains.

Saskatchewan – found in the mixed-wood and parkland areas north to Kazan Lake, Prince Albert National Park and Montreal Lake. In the south, they are found in wooded river valleys and tributaries.

Manitoba – breed across the southern half of the province, favoring moist woodlands in the east and mixed and deciduous woods in the west.

NESTING

Saw-whets prefer mixed-wood forests in the north, deciduous groves in the parklands, and densely wooded coulees and river valleys on the prairies. They are also found in dense alder thickets and tamarack bogs. Although they are considered to be a permanent resident in their breeding territory, some local movements may occur in winter.

The male Northern Saw-whet sets up his territory in early April. His night-long, monotonous series of whistled toots, reminiscent of someone sharpening or "whetting" a saw, have earned this species its name. The female incubates a clutch of white eggs.

NESTBOXES

Saw-whets will nest in a variety of habitats, though they seem to prefer deep mixed-wood areas. They will readily accept nestboxes, and often take up residence in boxes set out for Buffleheads and goldeneyes.

NORTHERN HAWK OWL

(Surnia ulula)
Eggs: *3-10 (13)*
Incubation Period: *25-30 days*
Time in Nest: *23-27 days*

Northern Hawk Owls are tame, medium-sized owls that resemble hawks in posture and flight. They have long tails, relatively short wings and no ear tufts. Their whitish faces are bordered with black "side burns", and the underparts are cross-barred in brown.

Northern Hawk Owls hunt extensively during the day. Mice, voles, chipmunks, snowshoe hares, small birds and insects constitute their diet.

DISTRIBUTION

Alberta – breed locally in the northern half of the province and southwest into the Rocky Mountains and foothills.

Saskatchewan – uncommon permanent resident in the boreal forest south to Montreal Lake and Bainbridge. Rare breeder in the parklands.

Manitoba – rare, found in coniferous and mixed-wood areas of the northern portions of the province. Southerly breeding areas include the Pinawa area and Riding Mountain National Park.

NESTING

Northern Hawk Owls tend to nest in northern muskegs and old burned areas, where nesting sites are plentiful. They will use the hollow tops of dead spruce and birch trees, natural tree hollows, abandoned woodpecker holes and the abandoned nests of birds of prey. The clutch of white eggs is incubated by the female.

During the winter, Northern Hawk Owls tend to wander into the southern parts of the prairies. They return north to their breeding grounds in March.

NESTBOXES

Nestbox use by Northern Hawk Owls is not known at this time. Boxes placed in muskegs or old burned areas will likely be the most successful at attracting them.

Ellis Bird Farm Ltd. would appreciate receiving any reports of them using nestboxes or other artificial nesting structures.

Northern Hawk Owl nestlings

BOREAL OWL

(Aegolius funereus)

Eggs: *3-6 (10)*
Incubation Period: *26-36 days*
Time in Nest: *30-36 days*

The Boreal Owl is a small, brownish-gray nocturnal owl with a large head and no ear tufts. It has white underparts streaked with chocolate brown, white spots on its forehead and crown (rather than streaks like the Saw-whet) and a pale bill. The white facial disk has a distinct black border. The courtship song of the Boreal Owl is a rapid series of whistled notes, usually rising in pitch at the end.

Boreal Owls are nocturnal and feed on bats, mice and other small nocturnal mammals.

DISTRIBUTION

Alberta – breed in the muskegs, coniferous and mixed-wood forests of the north and central parts of the province south to Edmonton and in the Rockies from Jasper to Kananaskis Country and possibly to the Montana border.

Saskatchewan – uncommon permanent resident in the boreal forest, rare winter visitor in the parklands.

Manitoba – very rare. Prefer the Black Spruce areas of the northern boreal forests.

NESTING

Boreal Owls prefer to nest in old flicker and Pileated Woodpecker holes. The breeding season is from April to June and the female incubates the clutch of white eggs.

NESTBOXES

Nestboxes should be set out in over-mature mixed coniferous/deciduous forests or in deciduous stands that contain scattered clumps of conifers. Ellis Bird Farm Ltd. would appreciate receiving reports of Boreal Owls using nestboxes.

BURROWING OWL

(Speotyto cunicularia)

Eggs: *5-6 (1-11)*
Incubation Period: *28 days*
Time in Nest: approx. *35 days*

These small, ground-dwelling owls, also called Ground Owls, are distinguished from all other owls by their long legs and their habit of bobbing up and down when approached. The adults are boldly spotted and barred while the juveniles are buffy below. This coloration provides good camouflage in their prairie habitat. They are the only North American owl in which the female is not larger than the male. Adult females may be more heavily colored on the underside and often appear darker than the male.

Hunting over pasture land and cultivated fields, Burrowing Owls feed on mice, voles, grasshoppers, small birds, crickets, beetles and other small prey. Grasshoppers are the most common food of the young as they learn how to hunt. In the early summer, adults usually hunt at dawn and dusk, while at other times of the year they hunt mainly during the night. They may also be active during the day, but do not usually hunt at this time.

DISTRIBUTION

Before agricultural settlement in western Canada, the Burrowing Owl may not have been a very common breeder, because the open plains of the Alberta, Saskatchewan and Manitoba mark the northern limit of its distribution. It is thought that the population increased from the early 1900s to about 1950, probably because extensive cattle and horse grazing created suitable habitat. Since the '50s, their population has declined steadily. They are now listed as a threatened species.

The main contributing factors to the Burrowing Owls decline appear to be pesticide use and intensive cultivation brought on by increased mechanization. Some researchers feel that the owls probably suffered the greatest declines in the 1950s and '60s due to pesticide use and have never rebounded. Although most farmers are now careful with pesticides, low population numbers and accelerating habitat loss have prevented the owls from recovering to their former numbers. It should be noted that Furadan 480 Flowable®, commonly used to control grasshoppers, may be lethal to Burrowing Owls. The insecticide's label carries a warning that Agriculture Canada has placed a restriction on its use within 250 m (820 ft.) of nest burrows.

In addition to habitat loss and pesticide use, illegal shooting, road kills, predation, spring snowstorms and heavy rainstorms have also been contributing factors to the Burrowing Owl population decline. Furthermore, badgers and ground squirrels, which are the principal sources for owl burrows, are considered pest animals and their numbers have been reduced in many areas. Mortality during migration and/or on the wintering grounds may also be a factor. Despite extensive banding programs, it is not known where our Canadian Burrowing Owls overwinter.

Alberta – historically nested in an area outlined by Calgary, Wetaskiwin and Wainwright. The current range has shrunk considerably: in the eastern part of the province it extends north to Castor while in the west it extends westward to the base of the foothills and north to about Airdrie.

Saskatchewan – historically nested throughout the grassland areas as far north as Prince Albert and Nipawin. The current range is less extensive—as far north as Kerrobert, Saskatoon and Indian Head. Most common in the Cabri, Saskatoon-Outlook, Regina and Weyburn areas. The decline in Saskatchewan seems to be going from east to west.

Manitoba – historically common across the southern part of the province, but are now restricted to the extreme southwest corner.

NESTING

Burrowing Owls usually arrive on their breeding grounds in mid- or late April. In some areas within their range, breeding pairs live close together in colonies, while elsewhere they tend to nest singly. Owls will often stay in the same general area or use the same burrow year after year, as long as these are suitable for nesting.

Burrowing Owls require open areas with low ground cover, existing badger or ground squirrel burrows and abundant food. Pasture land and roadside ditches provide nesting areas, and the birds can often be seen sitting on mounds of dirt next to their burrows.

Although Burrowing Owls do not mate for life, some birds apparently stay together for more than one year. Once a pair-bond is established, the male modifies the burrow by digging and scraping out dirt with his feet, beak or wings. He then lines the burrow with dried plants, feathers and cow and/or horse dung.

The female incubates the clutch of white eggs. During this time, she remains underground and the male brings her food. Incubation often commences before the last egg is laid, so the young hatch at different times. Owlets begin to explore the area outside their burrow when they are 2 to 3 weeks old and begin to hunt for themselves at about 6 weeks. Once the young are active above ground, the owls may move to another burrow or use two or three burrows at the same time. This use of more than one burrow increases their chances of survival should the main burrow be predated. During late June and July, young owls are often observed standing around the nest burrow.

BURROWING OWL RESEARCH

Researchers are attempting to assess population dynamics of Burrowing Owls across the prairies. Dr. Joe Schmutz of the University of Saskatoon, together with Dan and Gwen Wood of Castor, have been working on a research project in Alberta since 1986. Through banding and observation, they are studying behavior, movement patterns and adult mortality.

Colin Weir and Wendy Slaytor of the Alberta Birds of Prey Conservation Centre in Coaldale are also actively involved in research and recovery programs. From 1986 to 1988, they spearheaded a provincial nesting survey in cooperation with Alberta Fish and Wildlife and the World Wildlife Fund. In cooperation with the Calgary Zoo and the Lethbridge Fish and Game Association, they have also initiated a captive breeding and release project using permanently disabled birds as breeding stock.

Research on Burrowing Owls in Saskatchewan is being conducted by Dr. Paul James of the Saskatchewan Museum of Natural History. Through banding and recapturing, and by examining productivity, pesticide and rodenticide use, predation and habitat changes, he is attempting to identify the causes of population decline.

Ken De Smet of the Manitoba Department of Natural Resources has been studying Burrowing Owls in detail in that province since 1987. Their population in Manitoba has undergone a very dramatic decline in recent years. By 1982, the population had declined to about 100 pairs. In 1990, the population further decreased to only 19 pairs, all of which were located in the extreme southwest corner of the province. In 1991, there was a slight increase to 23 pairs. In an attempt to increase the population, De Smet is gathering data on and banding the remaining birds. He has installed artificial nesting burrows, has attempted to protect existing nest sites, and has initiated a public education program. Since 1987, nearly 200 owls from Saskatchewan and North Dakota have been reintroduced into suitable habitat in southwestern Manitoba.

OPERATION BURROWING OWL

Since most Burrowing Owl nests are on private lands, landowner cooperation is a key factor in the species' conservation and recovery. Saskatchewan was the first province to initiate a private stewardship program, Operation Burrowing Owl (OBO), in an effort to address this problem. Launched in 1987, the program is managed in Saskatchewan by the Saskatchewan Natural History Society and is funded by World Wildlife Fund Canada, Wildlife Habitat Canada, Saskatchewan Wildlife Federation, and Saskatchewan Parks and Renewable Resources.

A similar program in Alberta was initiated through the Prairies For Tomorrow Program (a joint program of World Wildlife Fund and Alberta Fish and Wildlife Division) and the Alberta Fish and Game Association with support from Alberta Recreation, Parks and Wildlife Foundation, the Endangered Species Recovery Fund and the Environmental Partners Fund. In Manitoba, habitat is protected on private land through leases, or is voluntarily protected through cooperative agreements with the Habitat Heritage Corporation and the Critical Wildlife Habitat Program.

The goals of Operation Burrowing Owl are to protect and enhance critical nesting habitat and monitor wild populations through a program promoting and recognizing habitat stewardship practices by private landowners. The program also seeks to increase and maintain awareness of the Burrowing Owl as a threatened species and to improve habitat by installing nestboxes. Landowners with Burrowing Owls on their property are asked to voluntarily agree to maintain the owl's nesting area for five years. They are also asked to report the number of breeding pairs that return each year. In return for their help, landowners receive an attractive yard sign, a pin, an annual newsletter and recognition for their contribution. In Saskatchewan, a paid Habitat Conservation agreement is also offered to landowners with colonies of five or more pairs of owls on their land.

By 1991, there were 499 landowners enrolled in Operation Burrowing Owl in Saskatchewan, representing about 16,000 ha (40,000 ac.) of habitat. Data collected in 1991 indicated that there were approximately 650 pairs of birds censused through OBO, a significant drop from the estimated 1,092 pairs in 1988. Despite habitat conservation efforts, the population continues to decline.

In Alberta, approximately 200 landowners are participating in OBO. Approximately 19,000 ha (47,000 ac.) are being conserved under the program. A Burrowing Owl census in Alberta will be undertaken in 1993 and 1994.

The following organizations and agencies can provide further information about Operation Burrowing Owl:

Alberta
Alberta Fish and Game Association, 6924-104 St. Edmonton T6H 2L7. Phone: 437-2342

Alberta Fish and Wildlife, Non-game Management Unit, 9945-108 St., Edmonton T5K 2G6. Phone: 427-6750

Saskatchewan
Department of Parks and Renewable Resources, 3211 Albert St., Regina S4S 5W5. Phone: 780-9273

Saskatchewan Natural History Society, 1860 Lorne St., Regina S4P 2L7. Phone: 757-4476

Saskatchewan Wildlife Federation, Box 788, Moose Jaw S6H 4P5. Phone: 692-8812

Manitoba
Manitoba Department of Natural Resources, Endangered Species and Non-game Section, 1495 St. James St., Winnipeg R3H 0W9. Phone: 945-6301

NESTBOXES FOR BURROWING OWLS

Burrowing Owls readily use artificial nesting structures, which offer protection against predators and the weather, and allow easy access for inspection and banding. Until nestboxes were used, very little was known about the owls' basic breeding biology because of the inaccessibility of the nest chamber.

Plastic nesting structures, shown below left, can be made from about 2-3 m (6.5-10 ft.) of non-perforated 15-cm (6-in.) flex drain piping and an ordinary plastic bucket, about 20 cm (8 in.) high and 30 cm (12 in.) wide, from which the bottom has been removed.

The bucket, when placed upside down in a shallow excavation about 45 cm (18 in.) deep, forms the nest chamber. The upper end of the bucket will be a few centimetres below ground level. An entrance hole 15 cm (6 in.) in diameter must be cut into the side of the bucket. The flex drain pipe is then attached to this hole so that it serves as a tunnel between the nest chamber and the ground level. (For a double entrance, cut holes in two sides of the bucket and use two pieces of piping). If about one-third of the circumference of the piping tunnel is cut away and removed (see illustration) the owls will have a natural dirt floor to walk on. To exclude light from the nest chamber, install the the piping at right angles.

When the installation is complete, the excavation should be refilled and a piece of plywood placed over the open upper end of the bucket and camouflaged with a sprinkling of soil and weighed with rocks. To see directly into the nest chamber, lift off the soil and stones and raise the plywood.

Plywood nestboxes, shown below right, have also been used extensively, though the wood tends to deteriorate within three to five years. About 5 cm (2 in.) of soil should cover the floor of the box, which measures about 30 cm (12 in.) wide, 30 cm (12 in.) deep and 20 cm (8 in.) high. It should be buried at least 15 cm (6 in.) below ground level. Tunnels can be constructed from plywood or plastic flex drain piping. Follow the same installation procedures as described above.

At a distance of about 10 m (33 ft.) from the nest, put a 2-m (6.5-ft.) high post into the ground to serve as both a nest site marker and perching post.

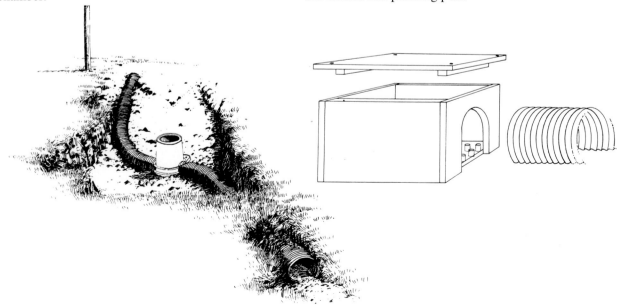

DESIGN, MATERIALS AND CONSTRUCTION

Because of their large size, nestboxes for the larger cavity nesters should be constructed for maximum durability. The nestbox shown here was designed by Jim Potter and Jim Allen of Red Deer, Alberta, specifically for ducks. It has been successfully field tested, so we highly recommend this plan for all the larger cavity nesters.

Use only 19-mm (3/4-in.) exterior grade plywood for strength and durability. Only two widths of material are required for this type of nestbox, which makes it easy to first cut the plywood lengthwise and then cut individual components. If an entire sheet is used, be sure to adjust specified measurements to allow for the width of the saw cuts.

DIMENSIONS

The habitat in which a nestbox is located, not the specific dimensions of the box itself, will most likely determine which of the larger secondary cavity-nesting species will take up residence. For example, Northern Flickers and several owl species will readily use boxes that are the same dimensions as Bufflehead boxes. For this reason, we suggest that four different box sizes will adequately accommodate all the larger cavity nesters.

HEIGHT

The height above ground at which a box is placed is not really critical; several species have been recorded using boxes placed at only 1.5 m (5 ft.). If given a choice, however, most species prefer high nesting locations. Since boxes placed closer to the ground are more subject to predation, disturbance and vandalism, we recommend that they be placed as high as possible, while still remaining accessible to the monitor. If you have climbing steps or are adept at using climbing spikes, try to put the boxes in the 4-6 m (13-20 ft.) range. If you are using a ladder, you will likely only be able to reach 3-4 m (10-13 ft.). If you do not have any climbing aids, try to put the boxes as high up as you can reach. Boxes will be most successful in secluded locations away from domestic livestock.

NESTING MATERIAL

The larger cavity nesters do not bring nesting material into the nest cavity, so straw or shavings should be provided. The depth of shavings in duck and owl boxes should be 5-8 cm (2-3 in.) while that in kestrel boxes should be about 2.5 cm (1 in.).

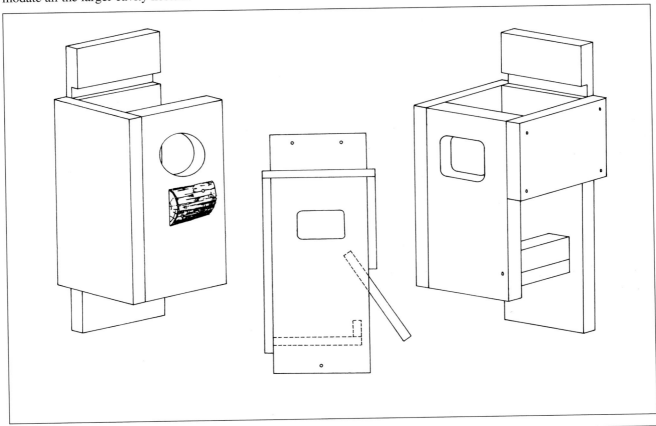

ASSEMBLY INSTRUCTIONS

Note: Use two nails at each joint to hold pieces together during assembly. Once the box has been assembled, fasten all pieces together with 5-cm (2-in.) rust-proof deck screws.

1. Fasten SIDE A to BACK flush with bottom of roof dado.

2. Attach FRONT to SIDE A, keeping the tops even. The ladder faces inside.

3. Attach shaving STOP on top of FLOOR.

4. Attach FLOOR 6 mm (1/4 in.) above the bottom of FRONT and SIDE A. This allows for a drip edge and makes the door easier to open.

5. Fasten SIDE B to FRONT and BACK.

6. Insert DOOR 1.3 cm (1/2 in.) up behind SIDE B (inside).

7. Hinge with one nail placed through FRONT and one through BACK into DOOR. Position nails 2.5 cm (1 in.) below SIDE B and 1 cm (3/8 in.) in from edge of FRONT and BACK.

8. To lock door, place a screw through DOOR into FLOOR.

9. Place ROOF into dado and fasten to BACK, SIDES and FRONT.

10. Fasten all SIDES, FLOOR and ROOF with 5 cm (2 in.) screws.

11. Stain or apply linseed oil to the outside of the box.

NESTBOX DIMENSIONS FOR LARGER CAVITY NESTERS

( ) denotes primary cavity nester not likely to be attracted to a nestbox. Primary cavity nesters described on pages 37-40. Dimensions are shown in inches/centimetres.

Box Size #1 Bufflehead; Northern Flicker; (Red-naped, Yellow-bellied Sapsucker); Northern Pygmy-Owl; (Black-backed, Downy, Hairy, Red-headed, Three-toed Woodpeckers)

Box Size #2 American Kestrel; Eastern Screech-, Boreal, Northern Saw-whet, Northern Hawk Owl

Box Size #3 Wood Duck; Barrow's, Common Goldeneye; Hooded Merganser

Box Size #4 Common Merganser; Barred Owl; (Pileated Woodpecker)

	BOX SIZE #1		BOX SIZE #2		BOX SIZE #3		BOX SIZE #4	
	Width	Length	Width	Length	Width	Length	Width	Length
Back	7 (17.8)	24 (61)	9 (22.9)	26 (66)	10.5 (26.7)	30 (76.2)	12 (30.5)	30 (76.2)
Front	7 (17.8)	18 (45.7)	9 (22.9)	16 (40.6)	10.5 (26.7)	24 (61)	12 (30.5)	24 (61)
Door	7 (17.8)	10 (25.4)	9 (22.9)	9 (22.9)	10.5 (26.7)	13 (33)	12 (30.5)	13 (33)
Floor	7 (17.8)	6.25 (15.9)	9 (22.9)	8.25 (21)	10.5 (26.7)	9.75 (24.8)	12 (30.5)	11.25 (28.6)
Stop	7 (17.8)	3 (7.6)	9 (22.9)	3 (7.6)	10.5 (26.7)	3 (7.6)	12 (30.5)	3 (7.6)
Side A	8.5 (21.7)	18 (45.7)	10.5 (26.7)	16 (40.6)	12 (30.5)	24 (61)	13.5 (34.4)	24 (61)
Side B	8.5 (21.7)	9 (22.8)	10.5 (26.7)	8 (20.3)	12 (30.5)	12 (30.5)	13.5 (34.4)	12 (30.5)
Roof	8.5 (21.7)	11 (27.9)	10.5 (26.7)	12 (30.5)	12 (30.5)	15 (38.1)	13.5 (34.4)	15 (38.1)

ENTRANCE HOLE SIZES

The top of the entrance hole should be 7.6 cm to 10 cm (3 - 4 in.) below the roof.

Circular
2 in. (5.1 cm) Downy, Red-Headed Woodpecker; Red-naped, Yellow-bellied Sapsucker
2.5 in. (6.3 cm) Northern Flicker; Hairy, Black-backed, Three-toed Woodpecker; Pygmy-Owl
3 in. (7.6 cm) American Kestrel; Boreal, Saw-whet, Northern Hawk, Screech-Owl
Rectangular
3 x 2.5 in. (7.6 x 6.3 cm) Bufflehead
4 x 3 in. (10.5 x 7.6 cm) Wood Duck
4.5 x 3.5 in. (11.4 x 8.9 cm) Barrow's, Common Goldeneye, Hooded Merganser; Pileated Woodpecker
5 x 4 in. (12.7 x 10.1 cm) Common Merganser
Square (rounded top)
7 x 7 in. (17.8 x 17.8 cm) Barred Owl (see page 28 for details and diagram)

Woodpeckers belong to a family of arboreal birds with distinctive physical and social characteristics, the Picidae. Most woodpecker species spend much of their life alone or in pairs eating insects found on or in the branches and trunks of trees. They have short legs and long, strong toes with sharp, curved nails. Their stiff, pointed bills are used in a chisel-like fashion to peck into bark, excavate a nesting site or to drum during courtship. Long, extendible tongues, which are barbed or sticky at the end, assist in extracting insects, while bristles above their nostrils filter out the dust raised by drilling. Their thick skulls are designed to absorb the shock of constant pounding. Most woodpeckers have a characteristic undulating flight.

PRIMARY CAVITY NESTERS

Woodpeckers are referred to as primary cavity nesters. The adaptations outlined above enable them to excavate new cavities each year. Because of their excavating ability, most woodpeckers, with the exception of the Northern Flicker, rarely nest in existing cavities or nestboxes. Nestbox plans for woodpeckers are shown on pages 35-36.

NORTHERN FLICKER

(Colaptes auratus)
Eggs: *6-8 (3-14)*
Incubation Period: *11-12 days*
Time In Nest: *25-28 days*

This is our only brown woodpecker. There are two forms of flickers on the prairies: the Yellow-shafted and Red-shafted. The Yellow-shafted Flicker, which is the more common of the two, can be identified by its yellow feather shafts on the wings and tail, by the black moustache of the male and the red band on the back of the neck.

The Red-shafted form has red feather shafts on the wings and tail, and the males have a red moustache. The females do not have moustaches. Intergrades, which show a combination of characteristics including orange-colored feather shafts, are found throughout the range of both species.

The Red-shafted form is more common in the mountains and near Cypress Hills in Alberta and in the southwest corner of Saskatchewan. In Manitoba, the Red-shafted form and intergrades have turned up as rarities at Reston and Brandon.

Their sharp *flicker-flicker-flicker* cry distinguishes flickers from other woodpeckers.

Flickers feed on trees, where they find wood-boring insects, and on the ground, where they eat ants, beetles, caterpillars and worms. Berries form a part of their diet in late summer.

DISTRIBUTION

This species has adapted well to human settlement.

Alberta – widely distributed throughout the province, though restricted to wooded river valleys and coulees on the prairies. In northern regions, it is most commonly found at the edge of clearings in deciduous and mixed-wood forests.

Saskatchewan – found across the province, especially common in the parkland belt.

Manitoba – widely distributed throughout the province.

NESTING

Most flickers return to the prairies in late March or early April, often to the same area each year, and often to the same tree to excavate a new nest. Their ranges are approximately 1.3 km^2 (0.5 mi.^{2}), but the consistently defended territory consists of only the area around the nest site. After the egg-laying phase, territorial conflicts usually occur in the immediate vicinity of the nest. Flickers usually mate for life, and greet each other upon arrival on the breeding ground with drumming and a distinctive *kekeke* call. This brings the pair together, and once bonded, they commence other courtship activities.

Since they are weak excavators, flickers tend to make their cavities in dead trees that are partially weathered. Although both male and female help in making the nest, the male does most of the work. Once egg laying commences, one adult remains in the vicinity of the nest site at all times. Certain spots near the nest take on special importance as preening and resting sites. The male and female both share incubation duties, though only the male stays on the nest at night. He also broods the young at night for the first few days after hatching. The nestlings are fed by both parents through regurgitation and are strong enough to crawl up to the entrance hole by the end of the third week. They are strong fliers upon leaving the nest, but stay with the parents for two to three weeks after fledging. By late summer, groups can be seen feeding in trees or on the ground. Most migrate south in September to mid-October, although a few overwinter each year.

Flicker nestlings

NESTBOXES FOR NORTHERN FLICKERS

If a pair of flickers find a cavity or nestbox to their liking, they are likely to return to it year after year.

Flickers tend to prefer boxes that resemble natural cavities. For this reason, slab boxes or boxes made out of tree stumps are the most favored. The nestbox plan for ducks, kestrels and owls shown on page 35 can also be used for flickers, though a slab of rough wood should be attached to the front. Other nestbox plans for flickers are shown below right.

Since flickers have a strong urge to excavate, they will sometimes damage the front nestbox panel. To prevent this from happening, stuff the box full of wood shavings and tamp them firmly. The birds will then "excavate" the shavings, which will satisfy their natural behavioral instincts without damaging the box. If it is not feasible to fill the box, cover the floor with shavings to a few centimetres in depth to protect and insulate the eggs.

Boxes should be located either within or at the very edge of a deciduous or mixed-wood forest. They can be mounted on poles or attached to trees. Starlings and squirrels will often compete with flickers for nestboxes, so frequent monitoring in the spring is important to prevent these competitors from becoming established. Disturbance should be kept to a minimum during the incubation period, which is a very sensitive time for flickers. Once the young have hatched, the box can be monitored regularly.

Flickers will sometimes enlarge the entrance on bluebird and Tree Swallow nestboxes, especially those made from cedar or other unprocessed wood. Some nestbox trail operators report that the male flicker will attempt to enlarge the entrance holes of adjacent nestboxes even after his mate has started to incubate in her own box. To discourage or prevent them from doing this, attach a metal protector plate over the entrance hole (see page 17). You can also "paint" contact cement around the entrance hole. The cement, which seems to be distasteful to the flickers, dries quickly so is not a threat to any other bird using the box. Constructing a box out of 19-mm (3/4-in.) fir plywood will also help prevent damage because it is so tough to peck.

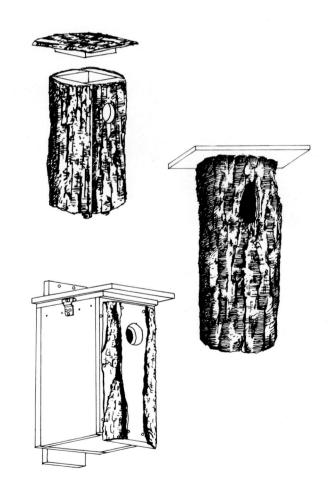

"Natural" flicker nestboxes

THE OTHER PRIMARY CAVITY NESTERS

The following primary cavity nesters are not likely to nest in nestboxes, but sometimes use larger boxes to roost in at night. All primary cavity nesters are important, both for the role they play in the forest ecosystem and because they provide nesting sites for secondary cavity nesters. Any reports of these other woodpeckers using nestboxes for either nesting or roosting should be documented.

RED-HEADED WOODPECKER
(Melanerpes erythrocephalus)

The Red-headed Woodpecker is conspicuous with its brilliant red head, neck and throat. This contrasts with its white underparts, white rump and black back, black tail and black upper wings. In flight, its large white wing patches are striking.

DISTRIBUTION

No breeding records in Alberta, very rare in Saskatchewan, uncommon breeder in southern Manitoba.

RED-NAPED SAPSUCKER
(Sphyrapicus nuchalis)

Red-naped Sapsuckers have red forecrowns and a variable red patch on the back of their heads. The male's chin and throat are red, while the female has a white chin and variable amount of red on the throat.

DISTRIBUTION

Breed in the mountains and foothills of Alberta and in the Cypress Hills of Saskatchewan. No breeding records in Manitoba.

YELLOW-BELLIED SAPSUCKER
(Sphyrapicus varius)

Yellow-bellied Sapsuckers have a red forecrown on a black and white head. The male's chin and throat are red, the female's are white. Their backs are black with a white rump, and they have a large white wing patch. Their underparts are yellowish.

DISTRIBUTION

Common throughout most of the wooded areas of all three provinces.

DOWNY WOODPECKER
(Picoides pubescens)

The Downy Woodpecker is our smallest black and white woodpecker. It has a broad white stripe down the back. The adult male has a bar of red at the nape of his neck. Downys can be distinguished from Hairy Woodpeckers by their small size, the faint dark bars or spots on the outer tail feathers and a very short bill.

DISTRIBUTION

Permanent resident across the central and southern parts of the three prairie provinces. They are most common in aspen groves.

HAIRY WOODPECKER
(Picoides villosus)

The Hairy Woodpecker is very similar to the Downy, but is much larger, has a much longer bill and pure white outer tail feathers. Males have a red bar on the nape.

DISTRIBUTION

Hairys are resident in all wooded parts of Alberta, Saskatchewan and Manitoba, where they are found regularly in the deciduous and mixed-wood forest portions of the central and southern parts of the provinces, including the prairie river valleys.

BLACK-BACKED WOODPECKER
(Picoides arcticus)

The Black-backed Woodpecker resembles the Three-toed, but has a solid black back. Only the males have yellow on their crown.

DISTRIBUTION

Breed in the coniferous forests of the northern and southwestern parts of Alberta, in the mixed-wood and boreal forests of Saskatchewan, and throughout much of the boreal forest of Manitoba.

THREE-TOED WOODPECKER
(Picoides tridactylus)

This woodpecker has black and white barring down the centre of its back and heavily barred sides. The males have a yellow cap.

DISTRIBUTION

Resident species that breed in the northern half and in the Rocky Mountain regions of Alberta, in the mixed-wood and boreal forests of Saskatchewan, and in the boreal forest of Manitoba.

PILEATED WOODPECKER
(Dryocopus pileatus)

The Pileated, our largest woodpecker, is unmistakable with its bright red crest. The male has a full red crest and a red moustache, while the female has a black moustache and a less extensive red crest.

DISTRIBUTION

Breed in the northern half, the Rocky Mountains and foothills, and the river valleys of the parklands in Alberta and Saskatchewan. Uncommon in the central and southern parts of Manitoba.

FLYCATCHERS

Members of the family Tyrannidae, the flycatchers, are so-named because of their habit of darting out from their perch to snap up an insect. Most species sit with erect posture, and have quite large heads, bristly whiskers and broad-based, flat bills. Nestbox plans are shown on pages 72-73.

GREAT CRESTED FLYCATCHER

(Myiarchus crinitus)

Eggs: 4-6 (8)
Incubation Period: 13-15 days
Time in Nest: 12-14 days

This is a rather large flycatcher with a bushy crest. It is dark olive above with a gray throat and breast. The sides of the lower breast are olive while the belly and undertail coverts are bright lemon yellow. The tail is long and rust-colored.

Great Crested Flycatchers inhabit mature deciduous or mixed-wood forests, frequenting more open parts and/or the edges of small clearings. They perch on the higher branches of trees from which they dart out to snatch dragonflies and other insects. They also feed on insects from or near the ground and from bark crevices.

DISTRIBUTION

Alberta – range is expanding. Confirmed breeding east of Edmonton, and several pairs have been sighted around Red Deer and in the Buffalo Lake area.

Saskatchewan – breed in the parkland/mixed-wood forest belt across the central part of the province and are thought to be the most common in the large aspen woods in the Duck Mountain-Yorkton area. They probably nest in small numbers north of Regina in the Qu'Appelle Valley.

Manitoba – common and widespread in mature deciduous woodlands in the southern parts of the province. They are also found throughout the boreal forest and parkland.

NESTING

It is thought that this species returns to the same site year after year. Upon arrival in the spring, the male establishes a large territory and is very aggressive to other males and to other birds that venture into his territory. Two males will even fight in aerial combat.

Natural cavities or old woodpecker holes are usually chosen as nest sites, but Great Crested Flycatchers have been known to build in such places as garden pipes, mail boxes, stove pipes, gutters, tin cans and shoe boxes.

If the nesting cavity is too deep, they will fill it with leaves, etc., to within 45 cm (18 in.) of the entrance, then build a cup-like nest about 10 cm (4 in.) in diameter. The material used in the cup consists of grasses, leaves, pine needles, moss, bark fibres, rootlets, feathers of grouse, cast-off snake skins, cellophane and onion skins. Yellowish-white to pinkish-white eggs, either blotched or streaked and lined with browns and purple, are laid. Incubation is done by both sexes. The birds usually leave the prairies in late August or early September.

NESTBOXES FOR GREAT CRESTED FLYCATCHERS

Great Crested Flycatchers are able to defend their nesting sites from the House Sparrow but not from the more aggressive starling. In areas where starlings are not a problem, use nestboxes with a 44-mm (1 3/4-in.) entrance hole. If starlings are likely to be a threat, use the smaller 40-mm (1 9/16-in.) entrance hole.

The best locations for nestboxes would be along the borders of deciduous woodlands or in areas where tall deciduous trees are numerous.

Ellis Bird Farm Ltd. would be interested in receiving reports of Great Crested Flycatchers using nestboxes in Alberta.

Swallows belong to the family Hirundinidae, which is composed of graceful, insectivorous birds that catch their prey on the wing. They have long narrow wings, short legs and small bills. Nestbox plans for swallows are shown on pages 72-73. Nestbox designs that may reduce House Sparrow competition are discussed on page 43.

TREE SWALLOW

(*Tachycineta bicolor*)

Eggs: 4-6 (3-8)
Incubation Period: 13-16 days
Time in Nest: approx. 21 days

Tree Swallows are sleek, slender birds with long pointed wings and glossy iridescent plumage. Their bluish-green upperparts contrast sharply with their white underparts. Juveniles are gray-brown above, white below and usually have a grayish breast band. Yearling females also have brownish upperparts. Tree Swallows are the only passerines (perching birds) in North America in which the female takes two years to gain adult plumage.

Tree Swallows are sometimes semi-colonial, and in the wild will nest in old woodpecker holes along wooded shores. Their small, weak feet are poorly adapted for walking on the ground, but are well-suited for perching.

Tree Swallows are aerial insect feeders, taking most of their food on the wing.

DISTRIBUTION

Tree Swallows breed throughout all three prairie provinces.

NESTING

Tree Swallows return in late April or early May, and claim nesting sites soon after arrival on their breeding grounds. Both adults vigorously defend a small nesting territory, usually less than 20 m (66 ft.) in radius. Courtship takes place in the vicinity of the nesting hole, where the male sings and performs courtship displays.

Nest building is done slowly and inconsistently. The average construction time is two to three weeks, with the female doing most of the work. The nest consists of a grass foundation and a cup that is lined with white chicken or duck feathers. Their attraction for feathers is so strong that, with a little patience, they can even be enticed to pluck them from your hand. One white egg is laid each day until the clutch is complete.

Egg laying and incubation are sometimes interrupted when the adults temporarily desert the nesting area. This desertion usually takes place on cool, cloudy days when there are few aerial insects available near the nesting site. Thousands of swallows may be seen at this time skimming over the surface of larger water bodies in search of insects. Surprisingly, this temporary desertion does not seem to affect the success of the clutch.

Only the female incubates, but the male does guard the entrance when the female leaves to feed. He accomplishes this by looking out of the box with his head and shoulders filling the entrance hole. Approximately 5 percent of males are polygamous (have two mates). Usually only one brood is reared per season, though renesting is common if nest destruction occurs early in the nesting season. A second brood may be reared on very rare occasions.

Across the prairies, the majority of the young hatch during the second or third week of June. They are brooded by the female for the first 3 days. Both parents share feeding duties, ranging as far as 1.6 km (1 mi.) in search of food. They frequently carry the fecal sacs over a nearby water body, where they drop them into the water.

The fledgling phase is virtually nonexistent, since the young are strong fliers as soon as they leave the nests. They do not return to the nest, but continue to be fed by the parents for one to two days in the vicinity of the nest. All of them then leave the breeding area and join other swallows to feed over marshy areas where aerial insects are plentiful. They will also roost communally in these areas. Tree Swallows usually leave the prairies by mid- to late August.

VIOLET-GREEN SWALLOW

(Tachycineta thalassina)

Eggs: 4-5 (6)
Incubation Period: 13-15 days
Time in Nest: 23-25 days

This species is often confused with the Tree Swallow. It can be identified by the white that extends above the eye and white patches that extend onto the sides of the rump. The female is duller than the male and juveniles are gray-brown above.

The diet of Violet-green Swallows consists entirely of insects taken in flight over open fields, from surfaces of small ponds and above canyon streams and forest tops. They forage at varying heights, depending on weather factors that affect the height of flying insects.

DISTRIBUTION

Alberta – locally common on the eastern slopes of the Rockies. They have increased in abundance and have extended their range in recent years along the Red Deer, Milk and Belly rivers.

Saskatchewan – considered to be rare, except around Eastend, where they are uncommon. With the exception of the buildings at Fort Walsh, they are confined to cliff-nesting sites in the Frenchman River Valley east to the Rockglen area in the south-central part of the province.

Manitoba – accidental. A few records or sightings, but no breeding records.

NESTING

Like other swallow species, Violet-green Swallows commonly nest around residential sites. They are sociable birds, and in the wild will sometimes nest in loose colonies where standing dead trees provide nesting sites. They will also nest without disagreement alongside Tree Swallows.

Violet-green Swallows arrive on their breeding grounds about the beginning of May. They build a nest out of weed stems, grasses and feathers in crevices of cliffs, holes in trees, under the eaves of buildings or in nestboxes. A single clutch of white eggs is incubated by the female. Unlike Tree Swallows, the young will return to the nest site for several days after fledging. Most leave the prairies by the end of August.

NESTBOXES FOR TREE AND VIOLET-GREEN SWALLOWS

Swallows are readily attracted to nestboxes, especially those set out by water bodies or in marshy areas where flying insects are plentiful. Boxes should be set out in mid-April. Since their territorial requirements are so small, swallows will comfortably nest 8-9 m (26-30 ft.) apart.

Swallow boxes should be placed away from trees to reduce competition from House Wrens and away from building sites to minimize House Sparrow competition. Some trail operators report that they have had success excluding most House Sparrows from Tree Swallow nestboxes that have a 25 mm x 40 mm (1 x 1 9/16 in.) entrance hole. Charles McEwen of New Brunswick reports success with his two-chambered nestboxes, shown here, that have entrance holes measuring 24 mm x 76 mm (15/16 x 3 in.). Contact Ellis Bird Farm for detailed plans.

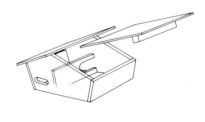

C. McEwen swallow box

Exit aids, described on page 10, must be provided because swallows, especially those weakened by hunger during a cold spell, may not be able to get out of a box unless footholds are provided.

Swallow nesting requirements are similar to those of bluebirds, so they often compete for nestboxes. Duplex boxes (see page 73) or single boxes placed in tandem about 6.6-8 m (20-25 ft.) apart will enable the two species to nest peaceably side by side. Where swallow populations are high, paired boxes may have to be placed as close together as 1 m (3-4 ft.). Keep pairs at least 90 m (300 ft.) apart. Since their diets and foraging habits are different, bluebirds and swallows do not compete for food.

PURPLE MARTIN

(Progne subis)

Eggs: 4-6 (3-7)
Incubation Period: 15-17 days
Period in Nest: 27-33 days

Purple Martins are North America's largest swallows and one of the most-loved of all backyard birds. Across the prairies, they rely almost entirely on human-made nesting structures.

It takes two years for both sexes to acquire their adult plumages. Adult males are entirely glossy purple-black and are the easiest to identify. Subadult (birds in their second year) males are often mistaken for females, but can be identified by a sprinkling of solid-purple feathers on their chins, throats, breasts, flanks and/or undertail feathers. Juvenile birds cannot be separated into sexes on the basis of plumage.

In spring and summer, subadult females can be distinguished by the weak blue to brownish color of their upper surface plumage. In adult females, this color is a much brighter, steel blue. During the summer, the distinction between the two becomes less obvious due to sun bleaching of the feathers.

Martins are completely insectivorous and feed on the wing. Contrary to what is widely believed, mosquitos do not form a substantial part of their diet (from none to at most 3 percent). Ironically, martins actually eat vast numbers of adult dragonflies and damselflies, the nymphal stages of which are the major aquatic predators of mosquitos. Theoretically, a martin colony should increase, rather than decrease, local mosquito numbers.

DISTRIBUTION

In North America, the range of the Purple Martin is generally bordered on the north by the boreal forest and on the west by open prairie.

Alberta – common in the aspen parkland, north to the Peace River district, east to the Saskatchewan border and south to Sundre. They rarely nest as far south as Calgary.

Saskatchewan – quite common, found as far north as Kazan Lake, Prince Albert National Park and Candle Lake Provincial Park. Absent in the southwestern part of the province.

Manitoba – locally common across the southern part of the province, although their range extends north to The Pas.

NESTING

Gregarious by nature, martins prefer to nest in colonies, and have taken well to apartment-style nestboxes put up for them throughout their North American range. It should be pointed out that a colony is not an assemblage of birds that travel or function as a flock. Rather, it is just a random grouping of birds attracted to a favorable breeding site. Colony members arrive and depart independently of each other.

Although very few now nest in the wild, the preferred habitat of Purple Martins was in open, mature woodlands with lakes, meadows or marshes interspersed among trees.

Data collected by Breeding Bird Surveys indicate that the Purple Martin population in North America increased between 1966 and 1986. Generally, martin populations increased in the southern and central portions of their range and declined in the north. It is thought that the major factor influencing population levels of Purple Martins is weather and, to a lesser extent, predation, parasites, nest competition and habitat changes. There are no well-documented adverse effects of pesticides on the species.

The migratory patterns of Purple Martins are weather-dependent, so vary from year to year. Their arrival at nearly all locations within their breeding range is a prolonged process, spanning 8 to 10 weeks in the north and 14 to 16 weeks in the south. Across the prairies, they usually arrive between the middle of April and the beginning of May. "Scouts," which are the oldest birds, return first. Scouts are very attached to the house they nested in the previous year, so arrive early to claim the very best nesting sites at their former breeding spot and to defend these against later arrivals. Once they arrive, the scouts do not return south for their "flock," as was once believed. Should a cold spell set in soon after their arrival, these early arrivals often perish from starvation. About four to five weeks after the scouts, subadult birds begin returning from the south, with the last of them arriving by mid-June.

When a female arrives at an established colony, each male remains near his own compartment(s), calling loudly. She inspects several compartments, and the male whose compartment(s) she chooses becomes her mate. Males defend the territory in front of their compartments before the females arrive, and even more vigorously so after pair-bonding.

Although only one nest is used, a pair will often initiate nest-building in more than one compartment. The nest is constructed by both members of a pair and is made of mud and a loose accumulation of plant material, grass, leaves, stems, twigs, straw and bark shreds. The upper surface of the nest cup is lined with fresh green leaves and/or leaf fragments that are plucked or torn from the outer branches of trees near the nesting site. The leaves are first brought in about the time the main nest is complete, immediately before egg-laying, and are continually brought in throughout the incubation period. Both sexes engage in this activity, but the male takes a more active role. The function of this adornment behavior is not completely understood, but is believed to reduce parasite numbers.

Martins are monogamous (have only one mate), but the males are extremely promiscuous and will commonly force copulate (mate) with females other than their own mate. Conspicuous copulations done in daylight elicit massive interference and attempted forced copulations by nearby males, so it is impossible for pairs to mate during the daytime near a colony. For this reason, it is thought that most pairs mate at night inside their compartments.

Once the nest is complete, a male will practise dawn-singing. This is an instinctual, distinct vocalization that is louder than any other vocalization, and is done in the pre-dawn and early morning. Although the reason for this behavior is not completely understood, Dr. Eugene Morton from the Smithsonian Institute theorizes that it is a strategy employed by the adult male to attract nocturnally migrating subadult males and females to the colony site. The male dawn-sings after his own clutch is complete. Once his mate has laid eggs, he no longer needs to defend her from other males because his paternity is assured and she is no longer vulnerable to forced copulations from competitors. He is then free to attempt forced copulations with other females. Dr. Morton suggests that dawn-singing is a beacon telling inexperienced, later-arriving subadult males that extra compartments, previously defended by the older birds, are now free for occupancy. These males will then attract subadult females as mates, with whom the adult males may try to copulate.

The female incubates the clutch of white eggs, though the male will insulate and protect the eggs and nestlings in the female's absence. Both parents tend the young. If outside temperatures are very hot while the young are still naked, the adults will sometimes soak their breast feathers by splash-bathing on the wing, then return to wet their brood. It is thought that this behavior helps keep the young cool.

The adults decrease feeding the young in the nest when they are about 26 to 28 days of age. Eventually, one of the young ventures out of the nest and attempts to cling to the sides of the nesting chamber. It is then mobbed by adult members of the colony and flies away, apparently to escape the mobbing. Harassment continues until the fledgling either perches on some object near (but not in) the colony, or flies approximately 180 m (590 ft.) from the colony. The female is in the entourage pursuing the young bird, but does not appear to participate in the mobbing. Eventually, after repeated short flights, during which it is mobbed again by adults, the young bird finds its way to a treetop some distance from the colony and remains there unless escorted somewhere else by the parent. This whole procedure is repeated with each nestling until the whole brood is brought together in a group, well isolated from the colony. The young then remain with the parents until they become independent, which usually takes another one to two weeks. The parents feed them during this time.

Adult martins do not recognize their young in the nest. As each offspring emerges from the nest, the adults key in on them and never lose sight of them until they find an isolated site away from the other mobbing adults. It is thought that it is at this point that there is first some type of recognition between parent and offspring. Mobbing behavior also drives the young away from the colony to an isolated spot where these recognition cues can develop. If this did not happen, the young would likely stay in the vicinity of the colony after fledging and solicit all adults for food. Driving them away minimizes the confusion at the colony site that this behavior might cause.

Some researchers hypothesize that this harassment behavior, which is usually carried out by yearling males, disperses the young birds before they have a chance to learn the location of their nest site. By forcing the young birds to disperse before they can imprint the location of the nest, the yearling males minimize future potential competition from these juveniles.

Martins usually raise only one family per season. When the young are strong fliers, they gather and start their migration southward. Martins are rarely seen on the prairies after the end of August.

The longevity record for a banded Purple Martin is 13 years, 9 months. The average life span is thought to be between 4 and 7 years.

ESTABLISHING A PURPLE MARTIN COLONY

Purple Martins will only be attracted to properly constructed housing set up in proper habitat within their breeding range. They require unobstructed air space for turning and landing, so houses should be set in an open area at least 12 m (40 ft.) from trees. No tall shrubs or vines should be allowed to grow on or under the support pole.

Research has shown that martin housing placed more than 30 m (100 ft.) from human habitation has a lower chance of being occupied. This is because martins have learned, through natural selection, that the closer they nest to people, the safer they are from predators. Martin housing should be placed in the centre of the most open spot available, about 9-30 m (30-100 ft.) from human housing.

The following techniques may increase the chances of establishing a colony: erect the house in an area with a sizeable pond or water body within 3 km (2 mi.); locate a new house near a neighboring colony site so that the overflow from the established colony can move into the new housing; use the same type of housing with which other landlords in the area achieve success; play tapes of martin calls in the spring; hang gourds from each corner of the house (see page 47 for more information on gourds); and put an old nest or smeared mud in a new house.

If a colony is already established, the house should not be put up until the earliest birds (scouts) arrive. Since it is the later-arriving subadult birds that start new colonies, newly placed houses should not be put out until 4 to 6 weeks after the scouts are expected to return to an area. An exception to this is if there are other active colony sites in the immediate neighborhood. In this case, some adults may be lured away from their previous nesting place if the new location is superior or if their old housing has fallen into disrepair. If the house is a new one, a few holes should be left open all summer, even if no activity is noted.

European Starlings, House Sparrows, Great Crested Flycatchers, Tree Swallows or even bluebirds will sometimes claim a martin house. This can be a problem if you are trying to establish a martin colony because the martins will be intimidated by other birds at a newly placed house. Once a colony is established, martins develop site-tenacity, so will usually successfully fight their way into that house the following year, even if it is occupied by other species. House Sparrows and starlings and their nests must be removed. Both of these pest species are persistent, so monitoring and nest removal will have to continue throughout the breeding season.

Charles McEwen of Moncton, New Brunswick, appears to have made a recent breakthrough in starling-proofing Purple Martin houses. He has found that a half-moon entrance hole (see below left), if cut to exact specifications, will exclude most starlings. The hole should be 7.6 cm (3 in.) wide and *must* be between 30.1 mm and 30.9 mm (1 3/16 and 1 7/32 in.) high. To retrofit existing wooden houses with starling-proof entrance holes, screw adapter plates over the old holes (see below right). The old holes must first be modified by enlarging them downward and outward because, in order to exclude starlings, the bottom, flat edge of the crescent opening must be placed 6.3-12.7 mm (1/4-1/2 in.) above the porch. Ellis Bird Farm would like to hear from anyone who experiments with these entrance holes.

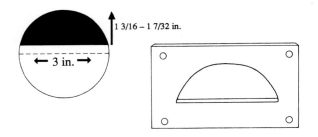

Although it may appear that House Sparrows and martins may share a colony house without incident, spar-

rows severely limit potential martin nestings by clogging numerous compartments with their nesting material. They will also build their nests on top of occupied martin nests and will puncture martin eggs and peck nestlings to death.

If a pair of Tree Swallows or bluebirds take up residence in a new martin house, encourage them to abandon it by plugging the holes and setting out several properly sized single boxes in appropriate habitat nearby.

Although martins have been known to nest in houses and gourds painted in other colors, they seem to be most attracted to white.

Ideally, a martin house should have extra perching areas in a neutral area away from the defended, private areas in front of each individual compartment. Perching rods located on the martin house roof work effectively. Some martin landlords supply additional perches by putting old TV antennae in the ground adjacent to the martin house.

Martin houses often have only partial occupancy because males often dominate more than one compartment. Occupancy can be maximized by inserting vertical dividers between compartments, thus allowing each male to defend only one hole. Dividers also prevent nestlings from venturing into neighboring compartments.

Some martin landlords suggest that occupancy can also be increased if the distance between holes can be maximized without decreasing the number of compartments. This can be done by designing a house that has one entrance per side (below left) or if the holes are placed as far over as possible to the left and right sides of side-by-side compartments, rather than in the middle (below right). Ellis Bird Farm Ltd. would be interested in hearing from martin landlords who use either of these design techniques.

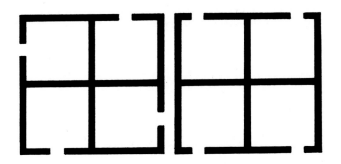

A martin house should have at least four compartments. Houses can be made as large as is desired by the landlord, though the larger they are, the more difficult and dangerous they are to raise and lower. The houses should be between 3 m and 6 m (10 - 20 ft.) off the ground. The pole on which the house is set should be planted firmly enough into the ground to withstand being buffeted by high winds. Setting it in a cement pad is recommended. Telescoping poles or poles operated by a pulley and winch are preferable to pivoting ones because they allow houses to be raised and lowered easily for box monitoring and clean out.

In areas where predators are likely to be a problem, the mounting pole should be equipped with predator guards. Use baffles or place a 1.5-m (5-ft.) sleeve of 15-cm. (6-in.) PVC pipe over the base of the pole.

Studies comparing aluminum martin houses with wooden ones have found that there is virtually no difference between the two. The advantage of wooden houses is that they tend to be cooler in hot weather and warmer in cool weather. The advantage of aluminum houses is that, being lightweight, they are easier to raise and lower. Aluminum houses also require less maintenance and last considerably longer than wooden boxes. Commercial aluminum houses tend to deter starlings because the compartments are so small, not because the walls are bright and reflective, as is sometimes claimed.

Charles McEwen of New Brunswick has increased the productivity of his martin colonies by insulating the floors in each compartment with a piece of 2.5-cm (1-in.) Dow styrofoam®. He scoops out a small cup-shaped depression in the material to accommodate the nest.

There is some debate as to the merits of porches and protective railings on a martin house. Some martin landlords claim that porches are a necessary feature of the house since they prevent the young from falling out of the nests prematurely. Others maintain that they encourage nestlings to engage in exploratory behavior outside of their compartments before they can fly. Research by the Purple Martin Conservation Association (PMCA) indicates that very few nestlings actually fall from the houses. Instead, they are deliberately knocked off by aggressive, older, unrelated colony members that instinctively try to make them fly by actually colliding with them, whether or not they are physically developed enough to fly. Railings do not prevent this instinctive aggression by other martins at the colony site. Since gourds do not have porches, baby martins do not usually venture outside of them before they can fly, unless the interior gets excessively hot.

Porches may also allow youngsters from one nest to crawl down the porch and get into a neighboring compartment. If they enter an empty compartment, they may starve to death. If they enter compartments with younger nestlings, they can dominate the entrance hole and steal all the incoming food.

Martin houses should be adequately ventilated, and should be constructed so they are easy to clean and store for the winter. All compartments should be easily accessible. If tier houses are constructed, hooks-and-eyes should be used to hold the tiers together.

The floor size of each compartment should be at least 15 cm x 15 cm (6 x 6 in.). Floor dimensions of 18 cm x 20 cm, 25 cm or even 30 cm (7 x 8 in., 10 in. or 12 in.) are preferable because they are roomier and allow the martins to build their nests farther from the entrance hole. This puts the young farther from the reach of predators and the elements.

The PMCA is currently experimenting to determine the hole size that martins prefer. In the meantime, they recommend a hole size between 4.4 cm and 5.7 cm (1 3/4 and 2 1/4 in.). Cam Finlay of Edmonton, who has also done research on Purple Martins, recommends a hole size of 5.4 cm (2 1/8 in.). Entrance holes should be placed about 2.5 cm (1 in.) above the floor. For martin houses plagued by starlings, try using the McEwen entrance hole (see page 46).

Gourds, whether natural, plastic or ceramic, are also used for Purple Martin housing in the USA, and are becoming more common in Canada. The most important feature about gourds is that they swing in the wind, which discourages sparrows and starlings.

Local garden centres can provide information about the only variety of natural gourd (Dipper or Bird House) that seems to be hardy enough to be grown in greenhouses at northern latitudes. Natural gourds should be treated with a preservative and then painted (only the exterior and the lip) with a white glossy oil-based paint. Unpainted gourds can overheat, causing the young to jump out prematurely. To preserve the gourds, dip them for 10 minutes in a copper sulphate solution (0.45 kg [1 lb.] sulphate in a 22.5 L [5 gal.] pail of warm water). Let dry several days before painting. Ventilation holes should be drilled into the lower neck and several 6-mm (1/4-in.) drainage holes should be put into the bottom of each gourd.

Perches should not be added to gourds, since martins are adapted to clinging vertically. Care should be taken when hanging gourds that they can only swing in one directional plane, either front-to-back or side-to-side. They should be spaced so as not to bump into each other.

Gourds can be cleaned by breaking up the mud that holds the nest together with the point of a long screw driver. The gourds can then be turned upside-down and the contents shaken out. They should then be washed out with a garden hose. If they are not cleaned out, a teaspoon of sulphur should be sprinkled in the nest to kill overwintering populations of martin fleas (*Ceratophyllus idius*). Gourds that are not cleaned annually tend to rot more quickly.

Martin houses can be inspected weekly during the nesting season without risk of abandonment. The houses should be lowered vertically and it is imperative that the compartments get properly reoriented to the same compass direction each time they are raised back up. If not, total disorientation of the parents can occur, and bloody fights may erupt over compartment and nest ownership. Since the adults recognize their own compartment but not their own young, innocent nestlings can get their heads pecked by rightful compartment owners when the nestlings' compartment gets shifted into a position where it doesn't belong.

If young martins happen to fall out of a nest, they should be returned as soon as possible. If it is impossible to reach the house with a ladder, use a long pole with a perch fixed to one end. The young bird will grip to the perch, and can be returned to its compartment. If a nestling is found to be suffering from malnutrition, it should be fed an emergency ration described on page 15. Pellets of lean raw ground beef mixed with boiled egg yolk, uncontaminated insects or high-protein, dry dog food pellets can also be used.

Crows and magpies may predate martin nests or catch the young martins on their first flight. Owls, especially Screech- and Great Horned Owls, have been known to take nestlings from the nest at night. Predator shields, like the one shown at right, are made out of hardware cloth and thin PVC pipe, and mounted to the outside of the house.

Predatory birds can also be deterred by attaching vertical dowel rods or heavy wire to the edge of the porches at about 6 cm (2.5 in.) intervals. Boxes with compartments at least 23-30.5 cm (9-12 in.) deep will put the young out of the reach of predators.

In addition to providing nesting sites, martin landlords can supplement their martins' diet with calcium by providing crushed eggshells and/or oystershell. Shells can be sun-dried, then put in a pail and crushed with a hammer.

They can be simply spread out on the ground or offered on a raised platform (make sure the platform has drainage holes). A metal pie pan nailed to the top of a 1.5- m (5-ft.) post set in the ground about 3-4.5 m (10-15 ft.) from the pole works well.

Nesting materials, including straw, small scattered twigs and a supply of wet mud can be supplied.

After the martins have left the nesting area, the house should be taken down and cleaned thoroughly. Used nests will be very dirty from excrement, some of which is deposited by older nestlings as they attempt to defecate outside the compartment. Pristine nests, which are extra nests or partial nests that were built but not used, should also be cleaned out.

Martins have the habit of picking shiny metal, especially pull tabs from aluminum beverage cans, and glass fragments off the ground and carrying them back to their nests. At the nest, they either incorporate these items into the structure of their nests or feed them to their young for grit. The young are not usually harmed by ingesting these foreign objects.

If a house remains unused all season, it should still be left up until early September so it may be discovered by adults on fall migration or juveniles looking for new sites.

Martin houses should either be stored for the winter or placed back up on the pole with the holes plugged until the arrival of the first birds the following spring.

PURPLE MARTIN ORGANIZATIONS
MANITOBA PURPLE MARTIN CLUB

This very active group, founded in 1980, has set out over 55 martin houses at senior citizens homes throughout Manitoba and maintains three large martin towers. The group produces four informative newsletters and sponsors several martin-related events each year. Annual dues are $8.00.

Contact: Ernie Didur, Box 36, Group 615, SS 6, Winnipeg R2C 2Z3. Phone: (204) 256-2079.

THE PURPLE MARTIN AND BIRD SOCIETY OF SOUTH EASTERN NEW BRUNSWICK

Founded in 1962 by Charles McEwen, this organization is dedicated to the conservation of all swallow species. Group members erect martin houses and distribute resource information. Mr. McEwen has produced a video about Purple Martins.

Contact: J. Albert Cormier, 54 Tower St., Dieppe, New Brunswick EIA 2G8.

THE PURPLE MARTIN CONSERVATION ASSOCIATION

The PMCA was founded by James R. Hill, III in 1986. It is dedicated to researching all aspects of martin biology and provides a centralized data-gathering and information source on the species. The PMCA publishes a colorful, highly informative quarterly magazine, *Purple Martin Update*, and has a mail-order catalogue of martin products. Proceeds help fund martin research.

In an attempt to coordinate the management efforts of all martin landlords in North America, the PMCA has established a colony registry program. Landlords who register in this program are invited to participate by filling out special annual colony report cards. Registered landlords are also invited to participate in long-term research projects.

Contact: PMCA, Edinboro University of Pennsylvania, Edinboro, PA 16444 USA. Phone/Fax: (814) 734-4420.

THE NATURE SOCIETY

The Nature Society was founded by J. L. Wade in the 1960s and is dedicated to Purple Martin conservation. The Nature Society publishes an informative monthly newspaper, *Nature Society News*, which serves persons who feed and house wild birds and other wildlife around their homes and yards.

Contact: The Nature Society, Purple Martin Junction, Griggsville, IL 62340 USA. Phone: (217) 833-2323.

The Canadian distributor for Nature Society products (including Purple Martin nestboxes and sparrow traps) is Eva Dannacker, Box 65, Main Post Office, Edmonton, AB T5J 2G9. Phone: (403) 435-0067.

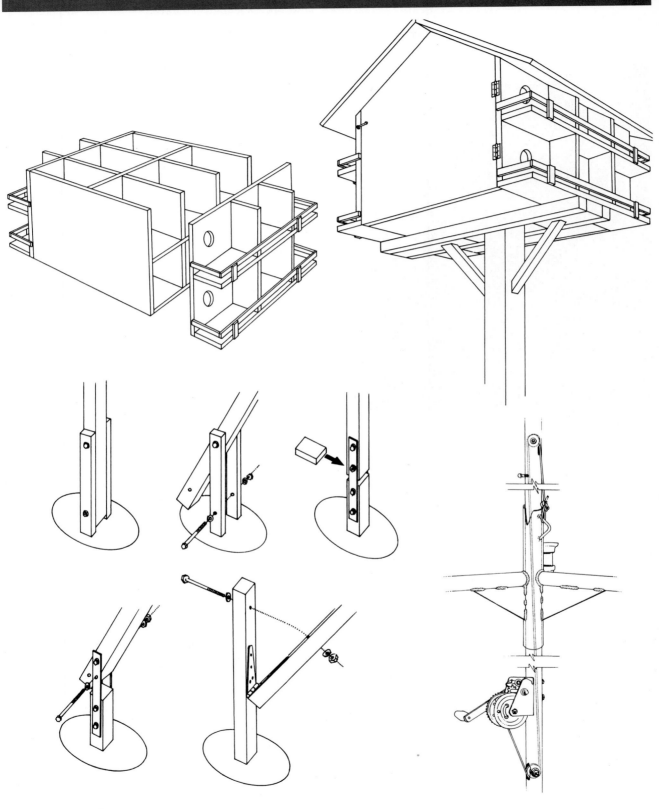

CLIFF SWALLOW

(Hirundo pyrrhonota)

Eggs: *4-5 (3-6)*
Incubation Period: *16 days*
Time in Nest: *23 days*

A squarish tail and cinnamon rump distinguish this swallow from all other prairie swallows. Adults have a dark chestnut and blackish throat and a pale forehead. Their backs are glossy blue-black with white streaks. Juveniles are much duller and grayer than adults, with a paler throat and darker forehead. Cliff Swallows are colonial nesters.

Cliff Swallows are insectivorous; they feed on the wing and will take insects from the surface of water bodies.

DISTRIBUTION

Alberta – widely but locally distributed throughout.

Saskatchewan – locally common in the prairies and park-lands, uncommon and local in the northern forests.

Manitoba – widespread and abundant throughout.

NESTING

Cliff Swallows arrive in small flocks in early May. Courtship activities are carried on simultaneously with early nesting activities, especially where pairs are involved in gathering mud for nest construction.

Cliff Swallows nest in colonies on cliffs, bridges, concrete dams or on the sides of buildings, especially under eaves. Using pellets of mud or clay, each pair builds a flask-like chamber that has a narrow entrance hole at the end of a short, down-curved neck. It takes approximately 1,000 mud pellets and about a week to build one nest. The nests are sometimes reinforced with straw and horsehair, but are generally quite friable and subject to erosion and breaking. Feathers and pieces of grass line the nest cup. The eggs, white spotted with brown, are incubated by the female. After the nesting season, adults and offspring of a colony stay together as a group. They usually leave the prairies by the end of August or the beginning of September.

House Sparrows will sometimes use Cliff Swallow nests, and have been responsible for the decline of the species in some areas.

CLIFF SWALLOWS NESTBOXES/STRUCTURES

Cliff Swallows will be attracted to artificial nesting structures, examples of which are illustrated on page 51. Because their nests harbour parasites, Cliff Swallows should be enticed to nest on barns or other out-buildings, not human residences.

SLATS – Unplaned 2.5 cm x 10 cm (1 x 4 in.) slats can be nailed on the side of a building to provide a base on which the birds can build their nests. The 10-cm (4-in.) side should be placed flat against the wall, about 15 cm (6 in.) below the soffits.

WOODEN NESTBOX– This nestbox consists of two stacked compartments with a removeable, sloping front. Although dimensions are not critical, it should measure approximately 30 cm (12 in.) high, 14 cm (5 1/2 in.) wide and 14 cm (5 1/2 in.) deep. Because of the sloped front, the roof measures about 14 cm x 18 cm (5 1/2 x 7 in.). The entrance holes should be 3.8 cm (1 1/2 in.). Smear clay around the inside of each compartment and mold it around the outside of the entrance holes to provide a base upon which the birds can build a neck. Grass should be put into each compartment.

CLAY/MESH CAVITY – This nesting structure was designed by G. Hamel of Deschambault, Quebec. It is constructed by mounting chicken wire on a piece of 19-mm (3/4-in.) plywood that measures 30 cm x 23 cm (12 x 9 in.). Cut two rectangular holes (9 cm x 14 cm [3 1/2 x 5 1/2 in.]) out of the plywood, then shape the chicken wire around each hole to a depth of about 9 cm (3 1/2 in.). An entrance hole of about 5 cm (2 in.) should be fashioned in the front. Finally, cover both the inside and outside of the wire cage with clay. The birds will finish the nest by adding mud to its neck.

In the fall, the mud that the birds added should be removed and the cavities cleaned. A stick can be put into each entrance hole to exclude sparrows and starlings. Remove them when the swallows arrive back in the spring.

CLAY MIXTURE

Mix 1 part pottery clay with 8 parts portland cement. Add enough water to make it the consistency of play dough, then roll it into small balls and press onto the wire mesh. Bits of grass can be added to improve bonding.

SLATS

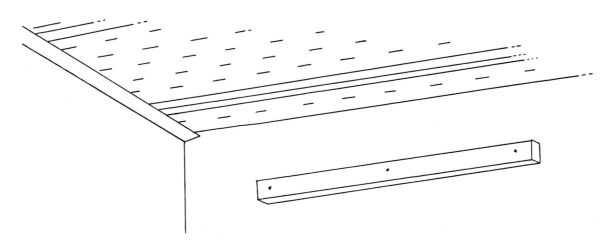

WOODEN NESTBOX

CLAY/MESH CAVITY

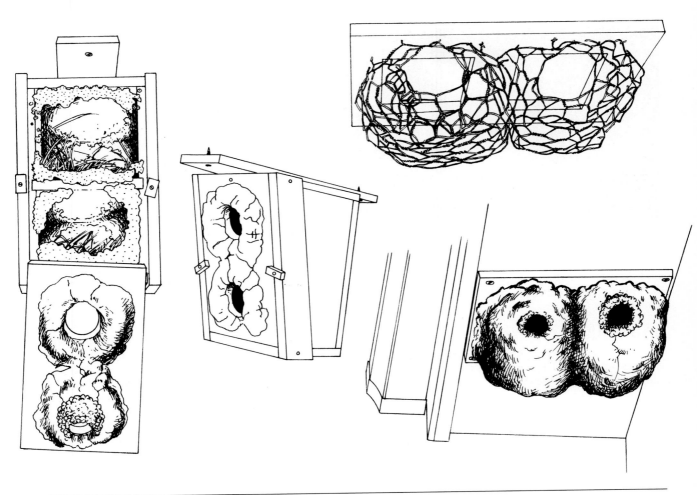

Chickadees belong to the family Paridae, small, tame, curious songbirds with short, stout, pointed bills and strong legs and feet. Chickadees spend most of their time roaming woodlots searching for insects and seeds amongst the limbs and trunks of trees, or on the ground. They are sometimes accompanied by nuthatches, kinglets, woodpeckers and/or migrating warblers and vireos. They readily come to feeding stations.

Chickadees have quite an extensive vocabulary and keep in constant verbal contact with their mates or others in their winter flock. They also establish pecking orders, with the most aggressive individuals at the top of the hierarchy. For nesting, chickadees use either a natural cavity, a previously excavated hole, a nestbox or a hole that they excavate themselves.

The use of moss in nest construction will identify a nest as belonging to a chickadee, but both nesting materials and eggs are so similar among species that positive identification can be made only by observing the parent birds. At first glance, it may seem difficult to distinguish one chickadee species from another, but the following characteristics clearly identify them: **Black-capped Chickadee** has a black cap, black throat and white cheeks; **Boreal Chickadee** has a brown cap and brownish back and sides; **Mountain Chickadee** has a white eyebrow and pale gray sides; **Chestnut-backed Chickadee** has a rich chestnut back and flanks, and the white on the face extends down the sides of the neck. Nestbox plans for chickadees are shown on pages 72-73.

BLACK-CAPPED CHICKADEE

(Parus atricapillus)

Eggs: *6-8 (5-13)*
Incubation Period: *12-14 days*
Time in Nest: *16 days*

During the winter, Black-capped Chickadees are the most common species to visit sunflower seed and suet feeders on the prairies. They have a varied diet of insect eggs, larvae and pupae, weevils, lice and spiders. Much of their food in the wild is gleaned by foraging over twigs and leaves, under bark scales and in crannies.

DISTRIBUTION

The Black-capped Chickadee is a resident species in all three provinces. There is some seasonal movement into southern areas during the winter.

Alberta – breed throughout the province, though is restricted to wooded coulees and river valleys on the prairies. Found in a variety of habitats, including mixed-wood and coniferous forests, tall thickets of willow and alder, shrubbery and residential areas.

Saskatchewan – breed throughout the province, except perhaps in the extreme northeast corner. In the southern prairie and agricultural areas, it is restricted to wooded creek and river valleys and coulees, urban areas and farmyards.

Manitoba – common across the southern and north- central region to Thicket Portage.

NESTING

During the late winter months, the males give their *fee-bee* song as an indication that they are breaking away from the winter flock and establishing their own breeding territory. A pair will then break away completely and the male begins to courtship-feed the female. Each pair remains in and defends a specific territory of about 4 ha (10 ac.) while nest building is in progress. This territory decreases in size during the incubation and nestling phases, and disappears altogether during the fledgling phase.

Black-capped Chickadees will use natural cavities, woodpecker holes and nestboxes to nest in. They will also excavate their own nest cavity, usually in dead or dying limbs or trunks of aspen or birch trees. Both sexes excavate the nest, which may be located anywhere from 15 cm (6 in.) to 3 m (10 ft.) above the ground. The nest is made from a base of moss that is then lined with plant down, fibres, hair, wool, feathers and spiders' cocoons. The male feeds the female while she incubates her reddish-brown speckled eggs and broods the young for a few days after hatching. Both parents then share duties of feeding and fecal-sac removal. They continue to feed the young for about 10 days past fledging. The young then disperse and gather into small winter flocks with unrelated adult chickadees. These flocks are stable in membership and are aggressive towards the intrusion of other groups into their winter territory of 8-20 ha (20-50 ac.).

MOUNTAIN CHICKADEE

(Parus gambeli)

Eggs: *6-12*
Incubation Period: *14 days*
Time in Nest: *unknown*

During the winter, Mountain Chickadees descend to lower altitudes and move eastward. They dine on insects, buds, berries, seeds extracted from cones and, during the winter, will visit feeding stations. They often forage in association with Boreal and Black-capped Chickadees.

DISTRIBUTION

Alberta – resident of the coniferous forests of the Rocky Mountains.

Saskatchewan – only a few sightings, most at feeders during the winter.

Manitoba – no records.

NESTING

Like their cousins, Mountain Chickadees nest in natural cavities in trees or woodpecker holes. They may also nest under rocks in banks or in holes in the ground. They probably do not excavate their own cavities. Nest sites are usually low to the ground, but have been recorded at 24 m (80 ft.). Their eggs range in color from unmarked white to white with varying amounts of reddish-brown speckles.

CHESTNUT-BACKED CHICKADEE

(Parus rufescens)

Eggs: *6-7 (5-9)*
Incubation Period: *unknown*
Time in Nest: *unknown*

DISTRIBUTION

A permanent resident of the dark coastal coniferous and interior valley forests of British Columbia, the Chestnut-backed Chickadee is also found in deciduous woods and thickets, and burned areas.

Alberta – extremely rare. No breeding records, although the most probable nesting habitat is in the dark wet forests of Waterton Lakes National Park.

Saskatchewan – no records.

Manitoba – no records.

NESTING

The nest of a Chestnut-backed Chickadee consists of a thick foundation of mosses, strips of bark, grasses, down of ferns, and feathers. The cup is well padded with thistle or milkweed down and the hair of rabbits, cattle, deer or mice. The white eggs are speckled or finely spotted with light red, reddish-brown or brown.

BOREAL CHICKADEE

(Parus hudsonicus)

Eggs: *4-9*
Incubation Period: *approx. 14 days*
Time in Nest: *approx. 19 days*

Boreal Chickadees prefer conifer and mixed-wood forests, where they feed high in the conifers, extracting the seeds from cones. They also dine on moths, caterpillars, beetles, insect pupae and eggs. They will also visit feeding stations in the winter to feed on suet and pastry.

DISTRIBUTION

Alberta – resident of the northern and central regions and southwestern foothills. It is absent from the prairies but is often found in the heavily wooded river valleys of the parkland.

Saskatchewan – common resident of the mixed-wood and coniferous forest regions. Found as far south as Duck Mountain Provincial Park, but not found in Cypress Hills on west side of province.

Manitoba – found in the boreal forest region. Absent from the extreme southwestern corner, primarily because of the scarcity of conifers.

NESTING

Boreal Chickadees will nest in old woodpecker holes, natural cavities and nestboxes. If a pair decides to excavate their own nest in a dead tree, the female does most of the work. The base of their nest consists of moss, lichens and bark while the cup consists of hair and fur. Their white eggs are speckled or finely spotted with reddish-brown. While incubating, the female is fed on the nest or outside the nest hole by the male. The young are fed by both parents.

Note: The incubation and nestling periods for Boreal Chickadees are poorly documented. If you attract Boreals to a nestbox, you have a great opportunity to collect important nesting information. Ellis Bird Farm Ltd. would greatly appreciate receiving such information.

NESTBOXES FOR BLACK-CAPPED, MOUNTAIN, CHESTNUT-BACKED AND BOREAL CHICKADEES

Chickadees appear to be more difficult to attract to nestboxes than many of the other small cavity-nesting birds.

Nestboxes for chickadees should be placed at chest height within or at the edge of a poplar, mixed-wood or conifer forest. Nestboxes tend to be less attractive if they are placed in areas with an abundance of dead trees or limbs in which the chickadees can excavate their own cavity.

To maximize the attractiveness of a nestbox, fill it half-full with wood chips or shavings so the birds can remove them as if they were excavating the cavity. Since House Sparrows cannot enter a nestbox with an entrance hole size of only 29 mm (1 1/8 in.), the only competitors that chickadees are likely to encounter are House Wrens.

Chickadees seem to be quite sensitive to disturbance so should not be bothered during egg laying or early incubation. Monitoring the box during later stages of incubation or when the adults are feeding young should have no adverse effect on them.

Boreal Chickadee nestlings

Creepers belong to a family of tree-climbers, the Certhiidae. As befits their name, they spend most of their waking hours creeping up the trunks of trees. They have the interesting habit of flying to the base of a tree, working their way upward around the trunk to the top, then flying to the base of a nearby tree to begin again. They are very shy, retiring birds, so are often overlooked. Like woodpeckers, they have long, sharp claws and a stiff tail that props them against the tree trunk as they hitch themselves upward.

BROWN CREEPER

(Certhia americana)

Eggs: 6 (9)
Incubation Period: 14-15 days
Time in Nest: 14-16 days

The Brown Creeper is a small, drab bird that is well camouflaged by its streaked brown upper plumage. It has a white chin, belly and breast, a long, stiff tail and a slender, down-curved bill. Its call is a thin *tsee*.

DISTRIBUTION

Brown Creepers show a preference for coniferous areas and groves of spruce and pine in a mixed-wood forest. Because of their secretive nature, they are often overlooked, so are not as uncommon as is generally thought.

Alberta – breed throughout the central and western regions of the province.

Saskatchewan – confined to the mixed-wood forest regions.

Manitoba – uncommon in the coniferous and mixed-wood forests of central and southern regions.

NESTING

Brown Creepers have the unique habit of nesting between the loose bark and the trunk of a dead tree. Their nest, which is built by both sexes, consists of bark or grass stems and lined with mosses, spider web, root fibres and fine pieces of bark. A clutch of white eggs, variably speckled or spotted with chestnut-red, reddish-brown or purplish-brown is incubated by the female. The male feeds her during this time, both on and off the nest.

NESTBOXES FOR BROWN CREEPERS

Creepers have been known to nest in natural cavities and old woodpecker holes. Their use of nestboxes is poorly documented. A pair of these elusive birds may be attracted to a shallow nestbox, similar to the design shown here. About 5 cm (2 in.) of shavings should be put on the floor of the box. It should be placed on the side of a coniferous tree in a mixed-wood forest.

Ellis Bird Farm Ltd. would greatly appreciate receiving any reports of creepers using nestboxes or other artificial structures.

Nuthatches belong to the family of short-tailed acrobats, Sittidae. They spend the better part of their lives climbing down tree trunks and branches in search of food. Their name is derived from "nut-hack," a reference to the nuthatches' habit of wedging a hard-shelled nut into a bark crevice and then hammering it until it opens. Nuthatches often store food by stuffing it into bark crevices. Nestbox plans for nuthatches are shown on pages 72-73.

WHITE-BREASTED NUTHATCH

(Sitta carolinensis)

Eggs: 5-9 (10)
Incubation Period: 12 days
Time in Nest: 14-17 days

The White-breasted Nuthatch is blue-gray above and has an all-white face and breast, and brick red undertail feathers. The silver-gray or gray cap on the female is smaller than the jet-black cap of the male. Its coloration, larger size and lack of stripes on the side of the head distinguish it from the Red-breasted species.

Donald and Lillian Stokes, who have produced the popular *Stokes Nature Guides*, identify several nuthatch calls and songs: *ank ank*—given by both sexes all year to keep in contact or, if given in a series, may signify disturbance; *ip ip*—a higher, quiet sound issued between a pair when they are feeding close together; *werwerwer*—the

male's song, given from high in the trees in late winter or spring at the onset of courtship; *pheeoo*—a wheezy whistle, first rising and then falling in pitch, given when intense excitement is experienced between a mated pair.

White-breasted Nuthatches spend most of their time on tree trunks, gleaning insects and other bits of food that may be found under the bark. They are frequent visitors to sunflower and suet feeding stations.

DISTRIBUTION

Alberta – fairly common resident in the parkland regions of the province.

Saskatchewan – resident in the aspen and mixed-wood forests in a belt extending from the southeast to the west-central part of the province. It also nests in the forested parts of the Souris and Qu'Appelle river systems, and in the Moose Mountain area.

Manitoba – common resident in the southern part of the province. It ranges as far north as Swan River.

NESTING

White-breasted Nuthatches prefer mature deciduous woods that contain old trees and tall broken stumps.

Beginning in late winter, the male nuthatch begins to bring morsels of food to the female. This behavior increases in frequency as nest building and egg laying approach, but stops soon after the young hatch. The female does most of the cavity excavating, which is usually started in the rotted knotholes of large trees. Nesting materials consist of bark shreds, fur, wool, cow hair and feathers. The birds will sometimes wipe crushed insects on the bark near the nest hole or will stuff fur into crevices near it. This is thought to leave a scent intended to deter mammalian predators from finding the nest site.

White-breasted Nuthatch eggs are white with brown dots concentrated at the larger end. Incubation is done by the female only, though the male will often feed her during this time. Bits of food are often stored in bark crevices near the site. The young are brooded by the female for the first few days of life, and the male will bring in food for the entire family. Fecal sacs are regularly removed from the nest. The young continue to be fed by their parents for about two weeks after fledging. The family unit stays together until fall.

RED-BREASTED NUTHATCH

(Sitta canadensis)

Eggs: 5-6 (4-7)
Incubation Period: 12 days
Time in Nest: 14-21 days

The Red-breasted Nuthatch is smaller than the White-breasted Nuthatch and can be identified by its black eye-line, white eyebrow and rust underparts. The males have a black cap while the females and juveniles have a duller head and paler underparts. Their song is a soft nasal *nyaa-nyaa.*

Red-breasted Nuthatches glean most of their food from the bark of tree trunks and branches, but will also dart out into the air for flying insects, pick up seeds from the ground and pry open cones to get at the seeds. During the winter, they will visit feeding stations to dine on sunflower seeds and suet.

DISTRIBUTION

Alberta – resident throughout the northern and western coniferous and mixed-wood forests, and south and east along river valleys into the parklands. They are also residents in the Cypress Hills but elsewhere in the south they are only transients or scarce winter visitors.

Saskatchewan – breed in mixed-wood and coniferous forests of the north, west and central regions, also locally common in cities and the parklands. They are usually residents, but some may leave the northern forests during the winter.

Manitoba – resident in the central and southern part of the province, with the exception of the extreme southwest corner, where coniferous growth is sparse. During some winters, they leave the boreal forests—irruptions have occurred at Reston and Brandon.

It is thought that adult birds tend to remain in their breeding area year-round, while juveniles migrate south for the winter, returning again in April, often in the company of migrating warblers. Following a year of low cone production, it is likely that they move southward early.

NESTING

Red-breasted Nuthatches arrive on the prairies in mid- to late April, often with flocks of warblers and other small birds. A nest cavity is usually excavated in an aspen, cottonwood or spruce tree trunk. Old woodpecker holes and nestboxes are also used.

Red-breasted Nuthatches have the peculiar habit of smearing spruce or pine pitch around the entrance hole. Although the reason for this behavior is not understood, it has been theorized that the pitch may act as a camouflage or predator-deterrent. Some suggest that it evolved in more southern climates as a snake deterrent. Nesting material consists of grasses, rootlets, moss, shredded bark and plant fibres. Their eggs are white, peppered with brown and lavender. They are incubated by both sexes. Both parents feed the young and carry out the fecal sacs. The family leaves the breeding area in early July.

NESTBOXES FOR WHITE-BREASTED AND RED-BREASTED NUTHATCHES

Although nuthatches prefer natural cavities or abandoned woodpecker holes, they will sometimes use a nestbox, especially if a slab of wood is placed on the front. Boxes should be made of weathered lumber or slabs of wood with the bark still intact and should be placed in shady coniferous or mixed-wood forests. They seem to prefer boxes placed at least 2 m (7 ft.) high.

Wrens belong to the family Troglodytidae, small, active birds of brownish color with slender sharp down-curved bills and, at times, cocked tails. They are bubbly, rollicking singers. Nestbox plans for wrens are shown on pages 72-73.

HOUSE WREN

(Troglodytes aedon)

Eggs: 6-8 (5-12)
Incubation Period: 13-15 days
Time in Nest: 12-18 days

The Latin name for House Wren means cave-dwelling nightingale. One of our most common prairie backyard birds, House Wrens are easily recognizable by their small size and bubbly song.

As well as being a cheery nestbox inhabitant, House Wrens may also help to control pest insects. One of their main food items is tent caterpillar moths, which they dine on by the hundreds every day, especially when feeding young.

DISTRIBUTION

Alberta – nest throughout the province. Prefer habitat that contains dense thickets and available nesting cavities.

Saskatchewan – breed in the central and southern regions.

Manitoba – common and widespread in the southern regions. Found in the boreal forest and parklands.

NESTING

Males arrive in early May, a few days before the females, and begin establishing territories by singing from conspicuous perches. They also begin to lay stick foundations in one or several cavities within a territory. Nest building is very energetic, with males making hundreds of trips to fill the cavities with sticks. When the female arrives in the territory of an exuberantly singing male, she is coaxed into viewing the cavities that he has filled with sticks. Upon selection of a nest site, she lines the rough nest cup with a variety of soft materials that may include fine twigs, feathers, hair, wool, cocoons, catkins and strips of inner tree bark. She lays one reddish-brown speckled egg each day and begins to incubate the clutch after the second last egg has been laid. The male makes no contribution to incubating the clutch, though he will pass food items to the brooding female. The males keep a close watch on the incubating female and will scold loudly if the female is away from the box for too long. Once the young hatch, both parents are active in feeding the nestlings and removing fecal sacs. Fledgling wrens are fed by the parents for a week or two after leaving the nest. Family groups disband by midsummer and begin to move southward in early September. Most have left the prairies before the end of that month.

Some males are known to be polygamous. Once their first mate is a few days into incubation, the male may attempt to attract a second female to another nearby cavity. If a second female is successfully retained, she begins to lay a clutch of eggs with her last egg being laid near the time that the clutch of the first female hatches. The male then devotes his attention to feeding the young of the first female. At the time that the first brood is close to leaving the nest, the eggs of the second female are just hatching. He then switches his efforts to feeding the second brood.

NESTBOXES FOR HOUSE WRENS

Wrens are one of the most easily attracted birds and they are usually undisturbed by the presence of people. There are records of them nesting in old boots, holes in walls, lawn ornaments and in clothes that were left on the line to dry! To attract them, a box with a 25-32 mm (1-1 1/4 in.) diameter entrance hole should be built and placed adjacent to or within a treed area, preferably where there are thick shrubs. Boxes should be erected by late April.

Despite their endearing qualities, House Wrens are aggressive and have the unpopular habit of taking over more than their fair share of nestboxes. They will break each other's eggs and those of other species when competition for cavities is keen. They may also kill nestlings in a similar manner.

The best way to limit such confrontation is to limit the number of boxes placed in or near heavily wooded areas and to put boxes for other birds at least 9 m (30 ft.) away from treed or brushy areas. If they continue to pester boxes, move the boxes at least 30 m (100 ft.) out into open areas.

Bluebirds are members of the thrush family, Muscicapidae. All members of this family are eloquent songsters. They have narrow notched bills and feed on insects and fruit. Nestbox plans for bluebirds are shown on pages 72-73.

EASTERN BLUEBIRD

(Sialia sialis)

Eggs: 4-6 (3-7)
Incubation Period: 12-14 days
Time in Nest: 17-22 days

The Eastern Bluebird has a distinctive chestnut-red throat, sides of neck, breast, sides and flank. Its belly and undertail coverts are white. The male is uniformly deep blue above while the female is grayer.

DISTRIBUTION

The Eastern Bluebird has followed agriculture's westward development. They were first reported in Manitoba in the mid-1880s and by 1922 had spread westward through Saskatchewan to the Cypress Hills.

Alberta – a number of sightings have been made and a few nesting records exist, including one at Ellis Bird Farm in 1991. Ellis Bird Farm is documenting all occurrences of Eastern Bluebirds in Alberta, so would appreciate being contacted with any records.

Saskatchewan – were formerly more widespread, and have now been largely displaced by Mountain Bluebirds. They nest sporadically as far west as the Qu'Appelle Valley northeast of Moose Jaw, rarely to the north to the Saskatoon and Hudson Bay areas.

Manitoba – restricted to the southern part of the province, where they nest in the parkland and boreal forest areas.

Although still uncommon in Manitoba, records kept by Friends of the Bluebirds indicate that numbers are increasing.

Hybridization between Eastern and Mountain Bluebirds does occur, albeit rarely. Friends of the Bluebirds (see page 63) is documenting and researching this occurrence by banding all cross-nesting adults and their offspring, and would appreciate receiving any reports of hybridization.

NESTING

Eastern Bluebirds arrive in early April and leave in late September or early October. They usually raise two broods per season.

Since the nesting behavior of all three bluebird species is very similar, we have summarized Eastern Bluebird nesting in the Mountain Bluebird section.

WESTERN BLUEBIRD

(Sialia mexicana)

Eggs: 4-6 (3-8)
Incubation Period: 13-14 days
Time in Nest: 19-22 days

The male Western Bluebird has deep royal blue upperparts and throat, and chestnut sides, breast and flanks. The belly and undertail coverts are grayish. Most birds show some chestnut on shoulders and upper back. The female is brownish-gray above with a chestnut tinge to the breast and flanks.

DISTRIBUTION

Alberta – very rare; the few confirmed nesting records that exist come from the western part of the province.

Saskatchewan – no records.

Manitoba – no records.

NESTING

There are not enough nesting records of Western Bluebirds on the Canadian prairies to determine when they arrive here in the spring.

Where they are found together in other parts of their range, Western Bluebirds tend to dominate in the river valleys while Mountain Bluebirds tend to be more common in the upland and more open locations. Western Bluebirds also prefer to nest in boxes that are attached to trees. Mountain Bluebirds and Western Bluebirds have been known to hybridize.

Ellis Bird Farm Ltd. is documenting all occurrences of Western Bluebirds in Alberta, so would appreciate being contacted with any records.

Since the nesting behavior of all three bluebird species is very similar, we have summarized Western Bluebird nesting in the Mountain Bluebird section.

MOUNTAIN BLUEBIRD

(Sialia currucoides)

Eggs: *5-6 (4-8)*
Incubation Period: *13-14 days*
Time in Nest: *17-21 days*

The Mountain Bluebird is the only one of the three bluebird species that lacks the distinct red breast. The adult male has sky-blue underparts, wings and tail. His belly and undertail coverts are white. The female has brownish-gray upperparts and pale blue wings, rump and tail. In fresh fall plumage, the female's throat and breast are tinged with red-orange, which makes them appear quite similar to Eastern or Western females.

DISTRIBUTION

Before the settlement of the Canadian prairies, bluebirds were restricted to the areas of the prairie provinces where nesting cavities could be found: the Rocky Mountains, foothills, aspen parkland, and nooks and crannies in the steep badlands of dry, prairie river valleys.

With the settlement of the prairies, farming practices created a vast area of new and ideal bluebird habitat: shelterbelts were established around homesteads, pastures were fenced (the fence posts provided nesting cavities) and fire control allowed the aspen parkland to expand throughout the northern portion of the prairies. Farm machinery also provided nesting sites. The bluebird population increased with this additional habitat, apparently peaking in the 1940s. The cause of their subsequent decline was probably the result of a combination of factors, including weather (especially spring and fall storms), habitat loss and competition from the introduced House Sparrows and European Starlings.

Alberta – breed throughout the southern and central portions of the province. Although there are nesting records as far north as Fort McMurray, Lesser Slave Lake and the Peace River areas, the northward range appears to have shrunk in recent years.

Saskatchewan – uncommon and local in the badland areas of the grassland region, common but local in the parklands, and local and uncommon in burned-over areas of the boreal forest.

Manitoba – southwestern part of the province is the eastern limit of their range in Canada. They have been reported as far north as Churchill, but are more common in the south. They are rare in the southeast, but are common in the southwest.

EASTERN, WESTERN AND MOUNTAIN BLUEBIRD NESTING

The first bluebirds usually reach the prairies in mid-March, with peak movement occurring at the end of the month and in early April.

As soon as the males arrive, which is usually a few days before the females, they begin to establish a territory containing one or more nest sites. While abandoned woodpecker cavities or nestboxes are most often used, bluebirds have been known to nest in unusual places; they have been recorded using farm equipment, mail boxes, oil field equipment, pipes, cliff swallow nests, old robin nests, holes in clay banks and the inside ledges of out-buildings.

Recent genetic research has shown that, while bluebirds usually have only one mate per breeding season, the young in a nestbox may not all be the offspring of both "parents." This mixed parentage occurs when the female mates with a male other than her mate, or when a female lays her egg in another's nest (referred to as nest parasitism). While it has been established that bluebirds are occasionally polygamous, it has yet to be determined just how common this behavior is. Bluebirds may pair-bond for more than one year, but most have new mates each season.

Once a territory is established, the male bluebird tries to attract a passing female by singing. Interestingly, territories established along fence lines tend to be more linear than those established around a natural cavity. Territories are usually about 230 m (755 ft.) wide, though they may be as small as 60 m (197 ft.) wide in dense populations.

Pair-bonds are formed soon after a female arrives. By this time, the male has usually explored all potential nest sites and tries to entice the female to inspect them by exhibiting several displays and behaviors. These may include flight displays, wing-wave displays, bringing bits of nesting material in his beak to the box, entering and leaving a box repeatedly, or hovering in front of the entrance hole. It may take several days for the female to finally select a box, but once a site is chosen, the pair focus all their activities around it.

The male initiates courtship feeding soon after the pair-bond is formed and continues bringing food to the female until the nestling phase. Donald and Lillian Stokes, in their excellent book *The Bluebird Book* (Little, Brown & Company), describe this and other bluebird behavior in detail.

The male also follows the female closely while she builds her nest and hunts for food. He is usually present when she enters or leaves the nestbox. At times he will indicate—through calls, wing-waving or by bringing her food—that she should leave the nestbox. It is thought that this close attention may be to prevent other males from mating with her or to ensure that she can leave the nest when there are no predators around.

Nesting territories are defended by both sexes: the male defends territory edges against other males while the female defends the nest site against other females. Extremely aggressive males will also defend the nest site.

Nest building, which usually takes four to six days but sometimes takes several weeks, is done by the female, though the male may sometimes carry bits of material. Under the watchful eye of her mate, the female gathers up sprigs of grass, rootlets or strips of dry bark, usually two or three at time, to form a cup-shaped nest at the back of the box or cavity. In areas where pine trees are abundant, pine needles may also be used. They will even choose odd nesting materials—nests at Ellis Bird Farm have been fashioned from such unusual materials as cassette tape and tinsel! Feathers are occasionally used to line the cup. It is interesting to note that the male will sometimes go into the nest and remove bits of nesting material. For some unknown reason, this behavior seems to prompt the female to increase her nest-building activity. Some bluebird trail operators put bits of dry grass beside or inside a nestbox to encourage the female to build in it.

Egg laying usually commences a day or two after the nest is complete, though delays of a week or more have been reported. Once she starts to lay, the female lays one pale blue egg each morning until the clutch is complete. Egg color varies from quite dark to very pale blue. Approximately 5 percent of bluebird eggs do not have any pigmentation at all. Although these pure white eggs look unusual, they are fertile.

While the timing of first clutches varies from year to year, depending on the weather, most egg laying on the prairies is completed by early to mid-May.

Occasionally, nests with an unusually large number of eggs will be reported. These abnormally large clutches are probably the result of either egg dumping or the laying of additional eggs over ones that failed to hatch. It is estimated that about 10 to 15 percent of bluebird eggs do not hatch. Factors thought to be responsible for this include genetic defects, infertility, chilling or over-heating.

Once the clutch is complete, the female commences incubation. The delaying of incubation until the last egg is laid ensures that all eggs will hatch at approximately the same time. As is the case with most songbirds, only the female bluebird is able to incubate. This is because the down feathers on her breast fall out to reveal a brood patch, which is a patch of bare skin richly engorged with blood vessels. While incubating or brooding, this bare skin provides the eggs or young with the necessary warmth. The female leaves the nest at regular intervals to preen or to feed, and while she is away the male may sit over the eggs to protect them. Incubation is performed throughout the night and during much of the day, depending on the air temperature. On very hot days, the eggs will continue to develop even without the female incubating them. At night, the male will sometimes stay in the box, perched on the edge of the nest. Once incubation commences, the female usually incubates continuously, though she will sometimes appear to abandon the box for a short period of time. Unless the weather is extremely cold, this temporary desertion does not result in nest failure.

On the prairies, most first clutches have hatched by the middle of June. During periods of hot weather, the eggs may start to develop before the female begins to incubate, so hatching is staggered. Under normal circumstances, hatching takes place over a period of 24 hours. If an egg gets slightly chilled during the incubation period, the layer of mucus between the shell and the chick becomes very viscous, making it difficult for the chick to peck its way out of the shell. This delay in emergence may also account for the age difference in nestlings that is sometimes observed.

As the young hatch, the female carries the eggshells away from the nest to avoid attracting predators. She may also eat some of the shells.

When the young hatch, they are tiny, helpless and almost naked, and unable to regulate their body temperature. For this reason, the female broods them almost continuously

BLUEBIRD TRAILS ON THE PRAIRIES

The known bluebird trails established across the prairies before 1975 are shown by the solid lines on the map below. The general locations of extensive bluebird trails currently in use are indicated by the numbered dots, and if you travel these areas in the summer, you will see bluebirds! If you have established a bluebird trail of 100 or more nestboxes in an area not indicated, please advise Ellis Bird Farm so your efforts can be noted. To visit a specific bluebird trail, we suggest you first contact one of the groups listed on page 63. Please, enjoy the birds from the comfort of your vehicle—do not disturb the birds or go near the nestbox.

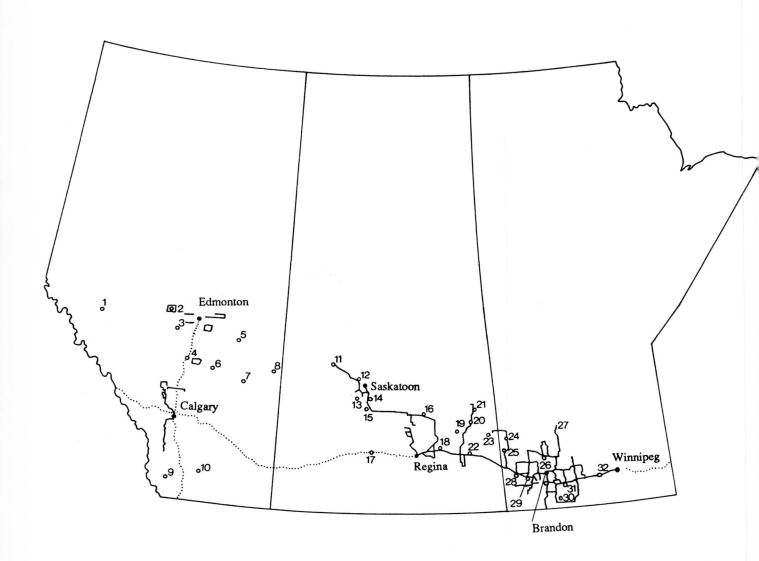

1. Hinton 2. Barrhead 3. Warburg 4. Lacombe 5. Viking 6. Stettler 7. Castor-Coronation 8. Provost 9. Pincher Creek 10. Lethbridge 11. Denholm 12. Langham 13. Delisle-Pike Lake 14. Dundurn 15. Hanley 16. Raymore 17. Caron 18. Fort Qu'Appelle-Indian Head 19. Melville-Waldron 20. Yorkton-Roxton 21. Gorlitz-Theodore 22. Broadview 23. MacNutt 24. Inglis-Russell 25. St. Lazare 26. Strathclair-Bethany 27. Ste. Rose du Lac 28. Hargrave 29. Oak Lake-Hartney-Souris 30. Ninette-Killarney 31. Holland-St. Claude-Austin-Carberry 32. Elm Creek

Saskatchewan and Manitoba historical trail information based on map by Donald S. Houston (Nature Canada 6 (2): 3-9 June, 1977). Used by permission of Stuart Houston.

Starlings belong to an Old World family of songbirds, the Sturnidae. They have long bills, which are yellow in the spring, and stubby tails. They are glossy in the spring and during the breeding season, and black speckled with white during the fall and winter. Short tails, direct swift flight and a hunch-backed appearance when walking distinguish them from North American blackbirds.

EUROPEAN STARLING

(Sturnus vulgaris)

Eggs: *4-6*
Incubation Period: *12-15 days*
Time in Nest: *18-22 days*

The first record of a starling in North America was a stray specimen found in Labrador in 1878. In 1890-91, several birds were introduced into Central Park in New York City by a group of ornithologists dedicated to the introduction of all the birds mentioned in Shakespeare's plays. The subsequent population explosion of this species across the North American continent can be attributed not only to the birds' adaptability but also to a lack of predators, habitat changes and the increase in nesting sites brought about by human settlement.

Starlings are highly adaptable, omnivorous birds whose food habits include voracious attacks on many insects.

DISTRIBUTION

Alberta – first recorded in Alberta in 1934, and now breed throughout the settled areas of the province. Some overwinter.

Saskatchewan – reached peak numbers in the '70s, but appear to have since declined. Some overwinter.

Manitoba – common and widespread. Some overwinter.

NESTING

Starlings nest in tree and rock cavities, buildings, caves and nestboxes. Their nests are an untidy accumulation of stems, leaves and plant material lined with feathers, moss or wool. Starlings have a well-developed sense of smell, with which they choose plants (eg. yarrow, rough goldenrod and wild carrot) that are toxic to the bacteria and insects found in their nests.

STARLING CONTROL

Starlings are aggressive competitors that will attack the eggs, young and adults of other cavity nesters. They also destroy fruit and other crops, and foul city buildings and yards with excrement when their numbers are high.

Fortunately for the smaller cavity-nesting species, starlings will be excluded from all nestboxes that have entrance holes 40 mm (1 9/16 in.) or smaller. They can enter through entrance holes that are 44 mm (1 5/8 in.) or larger, which makes them a problem in duck, owl and kestrel nestboxes. Sealing up such boxes for the winter, followed by weekly monitoring during the early part of the nesting season, is required to prevent starlings from using them. After the middle of April, most starlings will have found other nesting sites, so will not continue to bother the boxes.

Starlings prefer open areas and tend to shun dark, densely wooded areas, so nestboxes put within, rather on the edge, of woodlots will be less likely to attract them. They do not like to nest in gourds, and special entrance holes will exclude them from Purple Martin houses. See the Purple Martin section (pages 44-49) for details.

Starling traps, illustrated on page 70, can be used to reduce local starling numbers. The Webb, Mackay and drop traps can be modified for sparrow use and are described on pages 68-69. The Webb trap should be covered with 25-mm (1-in.) poultry wire, and the entrance hole on the nestbox should be 44 mm (1 3/4 in.). For detailed construction plans, contact Tom Webb (address on page 68). The Mackay multi-bird trap is a smaller version of the trap Charlie Ellis used for many years. It should be covered with 25-mm (1-in.) wire mesh and have a 44 mm (1 3/4 in.) entrance slot. If the larger, Ellis-style trap is preferred, contact Ellis Bird Farm for construction plans.

In-box traps, similar to the Kridler one described on page 69, can be used on larger boxes. For more information on this style of trap, contact Ellis Bird Farm.

WEAVERS (House Sparrows)

Weavers, commonly called House Sparrows and formerly called English Sparrows belong to an Old World bird family, Passeridae. They resemble, and are often confused with native sparrows.

HOUSE SPARROW

(Passer domesticus)

Eggs: 4-7 (8)
Incubation Period: 11-14 days
Time in Nest: 12-14 days

The male House Sparrow can be easily recognized during the breeding season by his black throat, bib and chestnut face-markings. The female is dull gray with an unstreaked breast and no distinctive markings.

House Sparrows are seed-eaters, but also feed on insects during the summer months.

DISTRIBUTION

House Sparrows are the most widely distributed land bird on the globe. They are widespread and abundant across the prairies, especially in urban areas and around farmyards. They are year-round residents, and nest in crevices, the nests of other birds (especially Cliff Swallows and orioles), holes in buildings, dense coniferous trees and nestboxes placed in urban areas or near farm buildings. They have also been observed building their domed-shaped nests among tree branches.

House Sparrows were first introduced into eastern North America by European immigrants between 1850 and 1870. Extensive propagation efforts, together with legal protection between 1851 and 1870, ensured the bird's survival and resulted in its subsequent explosive dispersal across virtually all of the settled portion of North America. In some areas, they preceded settlement by following railroad lines. In large cities, the House Sparrow population declined following the replacement of horse-drawn carts by automobiles; horse droppings had provided them with a major food source. Their numbers are now declining again in some areas in eastern North America where House Finches are increasing explosively.

While the decline of bluebirds and other native cavity nesters cannot be directly blamed on House Sparrows, the sparrows have exacerbated their problems by competing with them for nesting sites. Intelligence, aggressiveness, site attachment and year-round residency are characteristics that have helped this species increase and disperse so quickly.

NESTING

House Sparrows are not seasonally migratory, but flocks of 20 to 100 birds will move about within a 2.5-3 km (1.5-2 mi.) area.

The breeding season for the House Sparrow begins early in the spring or even in midwinter, and each pair will produce two, three or even four broods a season. Clutches of white, bluish or gray-green eggs spotted with brown are laid in a bulky nest constructed by the male and consisting of grasses, hair and feathers. Most nests are dome-shaped with a side entrance. The female incubates the eggs and the young are fed insects brought in by both parents.

A very strong bond develops between the male and the nest site he chooses. Spring courtship activities are designed to attract a female to the chosen site and to vigorously defend it from intruders. This site bond is stronger than the male-female bond, as evidenced by the male remaining on site even if the nest, eggs and/or female are destroyed or removed. This site attachment begins very early in the spring and continues, even if a pair-bond is never formed, through the entire breeding season.

House Sparrows will often take over a nestbox that is already occupied by a bluebird or Tree Swallow. In most cases, the bird inside the box is unable to defend itself against attack, so is killed by the male sparrow.

HOUSE SPARROW CONTROL

To some, House Sparrow control is seen as unnecessary and unfair. The argument used is that these birds are a wildlife species that should enjoy the same protection as other wild, nongame birds.

It is clear from the experience of the author and nestbox trail operators throughout North America that, unless some degree of control is exercised, especially on nestbox trails, House Sparrows will cause even further declines in the populations of some native cavity-nesting birds. House Sparrows are such a successful species that complete eradication will never be possible. If they are at least kept out of nestboxes, native cavity nesters, especially bluebirds, will be given a chance to increase their population levels. Charlie Ellis could not have brought back the bluebird to central Alberta if he had not been vigilant at House Sparrow control.

PASSIVE CONTROL

Passive control includes all preventative measures that discourage sparrows from becoming established in an area.

WINTER FEEDING - Just a few years ago, House Sparrows tended to shun sunflower seeds in favor of smaller seeds, cracked corn and bread crumbs. They have since acquired an appetite for these larger seeds, however, so will likely take over urban or farmyard feeders that offer them. If sparrows dominate winter feeders, the menu should be switched to canola (served from tube feeders with small portals) and suet. For more information on winter bird feeding, we recommend Ellis Bird Farm's publication: *Winter Bird Feeding - An Alberta Guide* (available at bookstores in Alberta or through Ellis Bird Farm Ltd).

ELIMINATION OF NESTING SITES - If the millions of nesting sites provided by the nooks and crannies of residential and farm buildings could be eliminated, the population of House Sparrows would decrease significantly. Although this is unlikely to occur on a wide scale, concerted efforts by individual property owners to seal up potential nesting sites can reduce local House Sparrow numbers. Old, unused machinery and buildings could be moved away from farm sites, and care taken to clean up spilled grain.

ELIMINATION OF ROOSTING SITES - During the winter months, sparrows are largely dependent on human-made structures for overnight shelter. Sealing up all buildings during the winter will encourage them to seek shelter elsewhere.

NESTBOX DESIGN - While a completely "sparrow-proof" box will probably elude us forever, efforts to design sparrow-resistant nestboxes are ongoing. Included here are some suggestions and designs that seem to be working in some areas.

House Sparrows can enter any box that accommodates bluebirds. Some trail operators report that most sparrows will be excluded from Tree Swallow boxes that have a small rectangular entrance hole. Success has been reported using either a 25 mm x 40 mm (1 x 1 9/16 in.) or a 24 mm x 76 mm (15/16 x 3 in.) entrance slot (see page 43). Ellis Bird Farm would be interested in hearing from anyone who experiments with these entrances.

In urban areas or around farm sites where sparrows are abundant, problems can be eliminated by setting out nestboxes for chickadees or wrens, since the small 25- or 29-mm (1- or 1 1/8-in.) entrance hole will prevent sparrows from entering them. Some sparrows can enter a 32-mm (1 1/4-in.) entrance hole. Be warned that, even though the sparrow cannot enter the box, he may harass the smaller species that try to use it.

Some trail operators in Kentucky have found that slot boxes seem to discourage House Sparrow and starling use. In one study, it was even found that bluebirds preferred slot boxes over the conventional boxes with circular entrance holes. Slot boxes have not yet been adequately field tested on the prairies, but are proving to be satisfactory in British Columbia. The slots should be 30 mm (1 3/16 in.) or 29 mm (1 1/8 in.) wide. A slot width of 30 mm is too small for starlings to enter, so should be used in areas where starlings are likely to be a problem. If starlings are not present, a 35 mm (1 3/8 in.) wide slot entrance can be used.

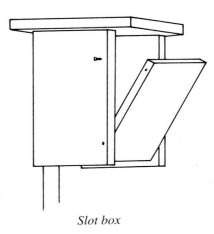

Slot box

Some experienced nestbox trail operators in Wisconsin feel that boxes with an open top most closely resemble the nesting sites that Eastern Bluebirds frequently use in old fence posts. They use mesh-topped boxes and have found House Sparrow use to be significantly less in these boxes than in conventional boxes. The Vince Bauldry design is shown here; prairie bluebird trail operators may want to try it on an experimental basis. Ellis Bird Farm Ltd. would appreciate hearing from anyone who experiments with this box design or requires detailed plans.

Vince Bauldry design

Where they have been field-tested, nestboxes made out of 10-cm (4-in.) PVC pipe seem to be unattractive to House Sparrows. They should be 30 cm (8 in.) deep and fitted with a 18 cm x 23 cm (7 x 9 in.) wooden roof.

It also appears that sparrows dislike wooden boxes shallower than 10 cm (4 in.).

Research done by the Purple Martin Conservation Association with natural gourds has shown that sparrows do not prefer them. This may be because Purple Martins prefer, while sparrows dislike, the swinging motion.

Trail operators have also observed that boxes with 6-mm to 12-mm (1/4- to 1/2-in.) ventilation slots, which admit light into the box, may discourage sparrow use.

Boxes should be sparrow-proofed during the winter to prevent the birds from claiming them in early spring. This can be done by putting a plug in (or over) the entrance hole, or by attaching a block of wood into which has been drilled a 25-mm (1-in.) hole, over the entrance hole. House Sparrows will inspect the box, but upon finding it too small, will probably not bother with it again. The block can then be removed when the bluebirds return.

In top-opening boxes with removable floors, the floors can be tipped up against the back of the box. This will keep mice out of the box and will transform the box into a non-cavity. Sparrows may inspect the box at some point during the winter or spring, but will conclude that it is worthless and so probably will not return to check it again, even when the floor is dropped back down. Removing the lids will also render them non-cavities.

NESTBOX PLACEMENT - Because sparrows tend to concentrate around buildings, it is safest to place boxes at least 1 km (0.6 mi) away from farm building sites or urban areas. In some areas, sparrow dispersal seems to be widening. In these cases, boxes may have to be moved farther into undisturbed habitats.

It has been suggested that sparrows will avoid nesting in low nesting sites if higher ones are available. Long-standing field tests have disproved this theory. Furthermore, boxes placed low to the ground are more susceptible to predation.

ACTIVE CONTROL

Once a sparrow has become established at a nestbox, active control measures must be used. Trail operators sometimes transport trapped sparrows and release them in another area. But this only moves the problem, it does not eliminate it. If you choose to do this, be sure to release them around farm sites or in an urban area where they are already plentiful. Do not release them in good bluebird habitat, or in areas where sparrows are not already well established!

Once disposed of, the sparrows can be frozen and given to wildlife rehabilitation centres, where they will be fed to rehabilitating birds of prey. If you cannot bring yourself to dispose of them, put them in a cage and take them live to a rehabilitation centre.

PROBLEMS AROUND BUILDING SITES

SHOOTING – Caution: this method should be carried out only when the strictest safety measures are followed. This control method can be employed year-round, but is best carried out during the fall and winter, when it can decrease the stock of breeding birds in a given area before the arrival of spring migrants.

CONTROLLING ROOSTING SITES – large groups of sparrows roost together in the dense cover of brush piles or clumps of evergreen trees, especially in winter. Shots from a powerful shotgun into these spots will no doubt eliminate some sparrows, but will ruin the habitat. Other methods, such as making loud noises or throwing objects, can be employed to drive them from roosting areas at dusk or shortly after dark. If they roost in machine sheds or other farm buildings, they should be caught or chased out at night.

TRAPPING – trapping programs, which should be employed on a year-round basis, are very effective at reducing local sparrow numbers. Several plans for traps that can be used for both starlings and sparrows are shown on page 70. Drop traps, which should be covered with 12-mm (1/2-in.) chicken wire, simply drop down over a flock of feeding sparrows and can also be used once the sparrows are coming into an area regularly to feed.

Multi-bird cage traps are very effective and easy to maintain. Several styles of these traps have been developed, with the Charlie Ellis-style probably being the most popular. For detailed construction plans of the Ellis-style trap, contact Ellis Bird Farm. Murray Mackay of Ponoka, Alberta, has developed a smaller, modified version of the Ellis-style trap. This trap measures .91 m (36 in.) wide, .91 m (36 in.) deep and 1.5 m (60 in.) high. It should be covered with 12-mm (1/2-in.) sandscreen mesh or chicken wire, and a 30 cm x 30 cm (12 x 12 in.) wooden nestbox should be placed on the ground inside or attached to the outside of the trap. This box serves a dual purpose—it offers the birds protection from the elements and, since they will fly into it when you approach the trap, makes it easier to remove them. Approximately 10 birds should be kept in the trap at all times to act as decoys. They can be attracted into the trap with grain, bread scraps, white proso millet, mixed bird seed or cracked corn. Water should also be provided. Since sparrows are gregarious, the success of cage traps depends on the birds being attracted to the food and to each other. Used continuously once the population is under control, its effectiveness, though varied throughout the year, is usually consistent.

The Webb trap, designed by Tom Webb of Turner Valley, Alberta, consists of a nestbox set on top of a wire cage. The floor of the box is made of thin metal balanced by a counterweight, so when the bird enters the box, it slips down into the cage below. The trap should be covered with 12-mm (1/2-in.) sandscreen mesh or chicken wire and the entrance hole should be 38 mm (1 1/2 in.). For detailed construction plans, send a stamped, self-addressed envelope to Tom Webb, Box 472, Turner Valley, AB T0L 0A0.

Multiple-bird traps are available commercially. Some of these have to be reset while others automatically reset, or are funnel-shaped and do not require resetting. Traps are sometimes available at hardware stores. The following is a list of mail-order suppliers. Please note that this list is for information only—endorsement is not implied.

HAVAHART – has an automatic elevator which resets itself after each sparrow is caught. Distributor: North American Bluebird Society, Box 6295, Silver Spring, MD, USA 20906-0295.

ST-1 – two compartments, needs to be reset. Manufactured by Nature House Inc. Canadian distributor: Mrs. Eva Dannacker, Box 65 Main Post Office, Edmonton, AB T5J 2G9. Phone: (403) 435-0067.

TOMAHAWK – has a funnel at each end that birds enter, no moving parts. Distributor: Tomahawk Live Trap Company, Box 323, Tomahawk, WI, USA 54487.

The Purple Martin Conservation Association also sells sparrow traps. For the association's address, see page 48.

All traps should be checked regularly in case a native bird happens to get trapped. If you are going away for more than a day, seal the trap.

PROBLEMS ON A NESTBOX TRAIL

DESTROYING THE NEST - Since the male House Sparrow becomes attached to a nest site, rather than to a mate, it may be difficult to discourage him from a nestbox once he has claimed it. If the female is removed, he will usually find a replacement mate. If she is frightened off the nest and the nest and/or eggs removed, she will usually abandon for another mate and site. The male will then rebuild the nest and attempt to attract a new mate. Continual cleaning of the nest material does not usually discourage an amorous male sparrow. The most effective way to solve the problem is to either remove the male sparrow or move the box.

If it is not feasible to move a box, plug the entrance hole or, if the box has a removeable floor, remove the floor for a few days. This may encourage the sparrow to leave.

One debatable method to discourage a male from using a box is a set mouse trap in it. The release action does not usually kill him, but will likely frighten him so much that he will not enter the box again. The mouse trap should be used only when it is certain that a male House Sparrow has claimed the box, and that no other species will enter it.

Observations by bluebirders in Kentucky indicate that sparrows will often abandon a box if their eggs are removed after the clutch is complete. This method appears to be especially successful in areas that are marginally attractive to them (i.e., away from farm buildings).

Some trail operators have found that boiling the eggs will keep a female occupied for most of the breeding season! Others who have tried this trick report that the female seems to sense something is amiss, so soon starts on a new nest.

Care should be exercised if a box is occupied by sparrows in close proximity to one or more occupied by bluebirds or swallows; if a nest is destroyed, a male may move to other boxes and kill the occupants. For this reason, it is especially important to remove the male sparrow from boxes located near bluebirds or swallows.

IN-BOX TRAPPING - The chances of trapping a male sparrow in the box increase as the nesting cycle progresses. Once eggs have been laid, the female can usually be caught on the nest at night. On rainy days, the male can often be caught in the box as well.

There are several styles of in-box traps that have been designed for use in nestboxes. One, designed by Keith Kridler of Texas and shown below, is a modified, portable version of the well-known Joe Huber-style trap.

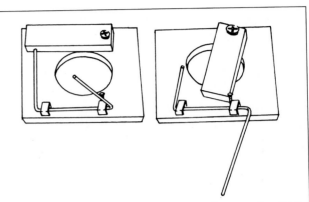

Use a piece of 6-mm (1/4-in.) plywood measuring 10.2 cm x 10.2 cm (4 x 4 in.) into which has been drilled a 48-mm (1 7/8- in.) hole. Make the trap door from a 76-mm (3- in.) long piece of 6 mm x 25 mm (1/4 x 1 in.) steel. Attach it with a short screw, allowing it to pivot down over entrance hole. The trigger can be made from 1.6-mm (1/16-in.) stiff wire (coat hanger wires or seismic flags work well). Each bend is approximately 63 mm (2.5 in.) long. Affix the trigger using insulated staples. Attach the trap to inside of the box using a screw or sticky-back Velcro® squares.

Joe Huber has also designed a box, called the Huber Trap-In-The-Box, that has a sparrow trap already installed. If you are interested in these traps, contact Mr. Huber at 1720 Evergreen Court, Heath, OH, USA 43055.

Walter Motyka of Edmonton, Alberta, has also designed a nestbox with a built-in trap. For more details contact Mr. Motyka, 9716-65 Ave., Edmonton, AB T6E 0K6.

The Peterson nestbox system has its own special in-box trap. To purchase a trap, or for plans, contact the Bluebird Recovery Program, Audubon Chapter of Minneapolis, Box 3801, Minneapolis, MN, USA 55403.

To remove the sparrow, hold a clear plastic bag against the entrance hole as you open it. The sparrow will fly into the bag. In-box traps should never be left unattended for more than one hour. The intent of these or any other trap is to capture House Sparrows so that they can be humanely disposed of, not to cause them suffering.

MACKAY TRAP

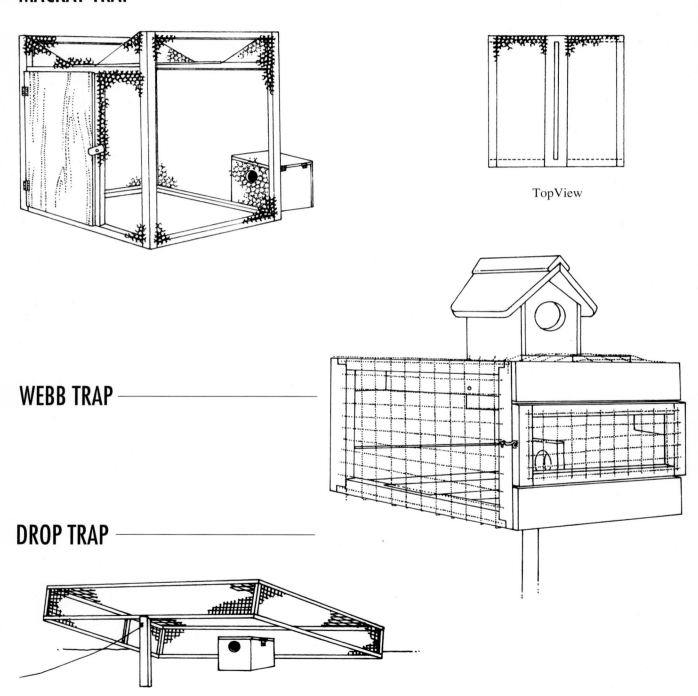

TopView

WEBB TRAP

DROP TRAP

FINCHES

Finches belong to the family Fringillidae, which is the largest bird family in the world. Their stout beaks and massive jaw muscles enable them to feed exclusively on seeds. Finches are well known for their beautiful singing and their erratic winter migrations. Plans for finch nestboxes are shown on pages 72-73.

HOUSE FINCH

(Carpodacus mexicanus)

Eggs: *4-5*
Incubation Period: *12-14 days*
Time in Nest: *15-18 (11-19) days*

The male House Finch has a dark red to reddish-orange crown, breast and rump. Its flanks are distinctively streaked with brown. The females are gray-brown above and whitish with brown stripes below.

Weed seeds are the main diet of the House Finch, though they also eat orchard fruit.

DISTRIBUTION

The House Finch is resident throughout much of its range. It is very common in both eastern United States, where it was introduced in the 1940s, and western United States, where it is native. Its range has been continually expanding over the last century. House Finches may be competing with House Sparrows for nesting sites in urban areas. There are also reports of House Finches competing with Purple Martins for nesting compartments. If it becomes established on the prairies, the House Finch will be yet another competitor for an ever-dwindling number of nesting cavities.

Alberta – very rare, may breed in the foothills between Calgary and Waterton.

Saskatchewan – very few sightings, first breeding record in 1992.

Manitoba – first breeding record in 1991. Although still rare in the province, there is speculation that the population will increase.

NESTING

The nesting habits of House Finches closely resemble those of House Sparrows. The finches will nest in a variety of places, including old buildings, nests of other birds, in large tin cans, nestboxes, on the ground, on ledges, among hanging plants, etc. They are both open-cup or cavity nesters and will sometimes take over the nests of other birds, even while they are still being used.

Nests, built by the female, consist of grasses, plant stems, leaves, rootlets, hair, string, cotton and wool. Their eggs are blue-white speckled with brown and black. The young are fed dandelion seeds. Two broods are often raised per season.

NESTBOXES FOR HOUSE FINCHES

Where they occur, House Finches readily take to nestboxes. The boxes should be placed under house eaves, on the limbs of low branches or on fence posts.

Used House Finch nests can be readily identified by the abundance of fecal material deposited around the nest cup.

Ellis Bird Farm Ltd. would be interested in receiving any nesting records of House Finches using nestboxes on the prairies.

Dozens of different nestbox designs have been developed and are being used successfully for bluebirds and other small cavity nesting birds. The following designs, which represent only a small sample of those currently in use, were submitted to us by veteran nestbox trail operators from across North America. They have all been subjected to extensive field testing and come highly recommended by the trail operators who are using them, and, in some cases, who designed them. Boxes are named after their designers or the groups who use them. Included are representative samples of top-, side- and front-opening styles.

The dimensions for the North American Bluebird Society standard top-opening bluebird design shown below left can be adapted to the other boxes. Because of its complexity, dimensions for the J. Potter box are also included. Plans for the D. Peterson box can be obtained from the Bluebird Recovery Progam of Minnesota (address on page 69). Three modifications that can be used on a top-opening box (hinged roof with weight, pivot floor and removable floor) are shown at bottom right. To review design/construction tips, see pages 10-11.

NORTH AMERICAN BLUEBIRD SOCIETY TOP-OPENING BLUEBIRD NESTBOX

Roof
7 1/2 x 8 in.
(190 mm x 203 mm)
Sides
5 x 10 in. [front]; 11 in. [back]
(127 mm x 254 mm/279 mm)
Front
6 1/2 x 10 in.
(165 mm x 254 mm)
Back
6 1/2 x 16 in.
(165 mm x 406 mm)
Cleat
6 1/2 x 1 in.
(165 mm x 25 mm)
Top Insert
5 x 5 in.
(127 mm x 127 mm)

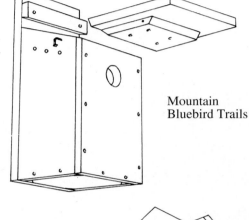

Mountain
Bluebird Trails

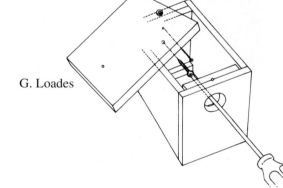

G. Loades

J. POTTER TOP/FRONT-OPENING BLUEBIRD NESTBOX

Roof
8 x 10 in.
(203 mm x 254 mm)
Cleats
2 x 5 1/2 in.
(50 mm x 139 mm)
Front Top
6 1/2 x 5 in.
(165 mm x 127 mm)
Front Bottom
5 x 6 1/2 in.
(127 mm x 165 mm)
Sides
6 1/2 x 11 in. [front]; 12 in. [back]
(165 mm x 279mm/ 305 mm)
Floor
5 in. x 5 in. (127 mm x 127 mm)
Back
5 x 18 in. (127 mm x 457 mm)

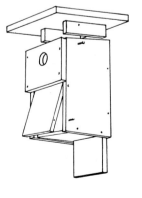

Modifications

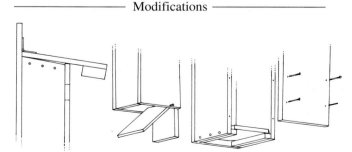

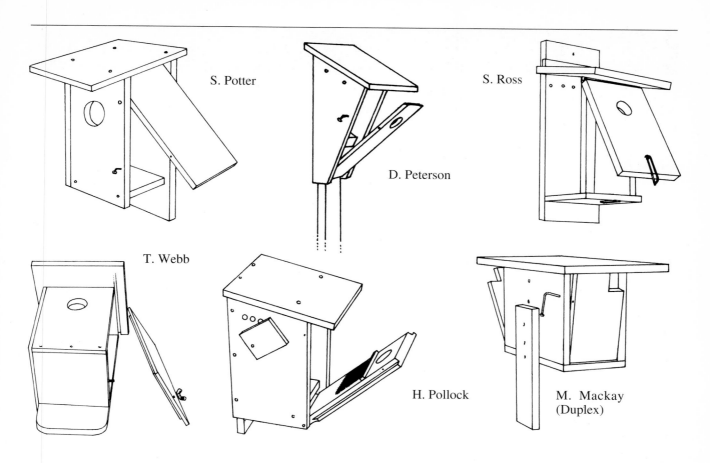

S. Potter

D. Peterson

S. Ross

T. Webb

H. Pollock

M. Mackay
(Duplex)

NESTBOX DIMENSIONS FOR SMALL CAVITY NESTERS
(measurements in inches with millimetres in brackets)

Species	Entrance Hole	Floor	Box Depth

Bluebirds
  Eastern
  Mountain
  Western
	1 1/2 (38)
	1 9/16 (40)
	1 9/16 (40)
		4 x 4 (101 x 101)
		5 x 5 (127 x 127)
		5 x 5 (127 x 127)
			10 (254)
			10 (254)
			10 (254)

Chickadees All Species	1 1/8-1 1/4 (29-32) 1 1/4(32)	4 x 4 (101 x 101)	8 (203)
Finch House	1 1/2(38)	5 x 5 (127 x 127)	10 (254)
Flycatcher Great Crested	1 9/16(40)	6 x 6 (152 x 152)	10 (254)
Nuthatches Both Species	1 1/2 (38)	5 x 5 (127 x 127)	10 (254)
Swallows Both Species	1 1/2 (38)	5 x 5 (127 x 127)	10 (254)
Wren House	1 - 1 1/4 (25-32)	5 x 5 (127 x 127)	10 (254)

Nests and eggs, clockwise from top right: Boreal Chickadee; House Sparrow; European Starling; assemblage of bluebird eggs showing color and size variations; Mountain Bluebird; Tree Swallow; House Wren; Black-capped Chickadee.

There are several species of birds that will be attracted to nest in your backyard if they are provided with a nesting bracket or basket. While these birds are not true cavity nesters, they are included here because they respond readily to the provision of artificial nesting sites.

BRACKET

Species that will be attracted to nest on a bracket include American Robin *(Turdus migratorius)*, Barn Swallow *(Hirundo rustica)*, Eastern Phoebe *(Sayornis phoebe)* and Say's Phoebe *(Sayornis saya)*.

Brackets should have a floor size of about 15 cm x 15 cm (6 x 6 in.) and should be placed under the eaves of buildings. Phoebes are most likely to use a bracket located near water.

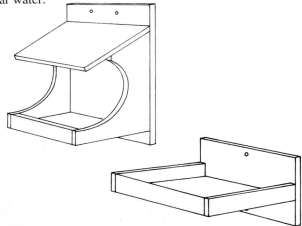

BASKET

Mourning Doves *(Zenaida macroura)* will often use 30-cm (12-in.) nest baskets constructed from 6.3-mm or 12-mm (1/4- or 1/2-in.) wire mesh. The baskets should be placed in the crotch of a tree limb about 2 m (6 ft.) off the ground. They can be fastened with nails or wire. The area around the nest cone should be free of obstructions.

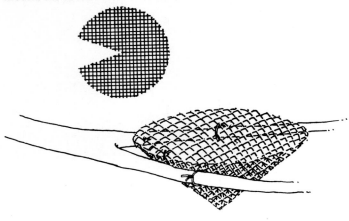

MODIFIED BRACKET

Eastern Kingbirds *(Tyrannus tyrannus)* are attracted to bracket-like structures. The one shown here, designed by Frank Lind of Rimbey, Alberta, basically duplicates the top of a broken stump, a site where these birds often build their nest.

The nesting structure consists of a small cage atop a 30-cm (12-in.) round block of wood that is 15 cm (6 in.) in diameter. The sides of the cage are about 7 cm (3 in.) high and spaced about 3.8 cm (1 1/2 in.) apart. They should be made out of thin plywood so that they can fit the contour of the block. The nesting structure is then attached against the southeast side of a tree using a 2.5 cm x 5 cm (1 x 2 in.) stave.

The nest brackets should be located at the edge of an aspen grove, preferably near water, and should be placed about 3.6 m (12 ft.) off the ground. At the end of the nesting season, the nest can be cleaned out by using a long wire with a hooked end. Just slip the hook under the old nest and flip it out.

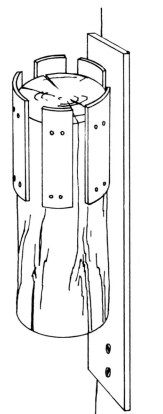

Named here are some non-government conservation groups across the prairies that may be helpful to nestbox trail operators. Also listed are nature centres, rehabilitation centres, provincial government agencies most directly involved with wildlife and/or conservation, and numbers to phone to report rare bird sightings. The section concludes with a discussion of banding, supplemental feeding, pesticides and sharing your backyard with cavity nesters. For a complete guide to Canadian environmental organizations and agencies, contact the Canadian Environmental Network (Box 1289, Stn B, Ottawa, ON, K1P 5R3. Phone: [613] 563-2078. Fax: 563-7236) for a copy of *The Green List.* Organizations dealing specifically with American Kestrels, Burrowing Owls, Purple Martins and bluebirds are listed under the species descriptions. Telephone area codes are: AB (403); SK (306); MB (204).

CONSERVATION GROUPS

NATIONAL

Canadian Nature Federation,
453 Sussex Drive, Ottawa, ON K1N 6Z4.
Phone: (613) 238-6154. Fax: 230-2054.

Canadian Parks and Wilderness Society,
160 Bloor St. East, Suite 1335, Toronto, ON M4W 1B9.
Phone: (416) 972-0868. Fax: 972-0760.

Canadian Wildlife Federation,
2740 Queensview Dr., Ottawa, ON K2B 1A2.
Phone: (613) 721-2286. Fax: 721-2902.

Ducks Unlimited Canada,
1190 Waverley St., Winnipeg R3T 2E2.
Phone: (204) 477-1760. Fax: 452-7560.

ALBERTA

Alberta Environmental Network,
10511 Saskatchewan Drive, Edmonton T6E 4S1.
Phone: 433-9302. Fax: 439-5081.

Alberta Fish and Game Association,
6924-104 St., Edmonton T6H 2L7.
Phone: 437-2342. Fax: 438-6872.

Alberta Forestry Association,
Suite 101, 10526 Jasper Ave., Edmonton T5J 1Z7.
Phone: 428-7582. Fax: 428-7557.

Alberta Native Plant Council,
Box 4524, Station SE, Edmonton T6E 5G4.
Phone: 438-1462.

Alberta Recreation, Parks and Wildlife Foundation,
7th Floor, Harley Court Building,
10045-111 St., Edmonton T5K 1K4.
Phone: 482-6467. Fax: 488-9755.

Alberta Wilderness Association,
Box 6398, Station D, Calgary T2P 2E1. Phone: 283-2025.

Beaverhill Bird Observatory Society,
Box 4201, Edmonton T6E 4T2. Phone: 465-2370.

Bow Valley Naturalists, Box 1693, Banff T0L 0C0.
Phone: 762-6320. Fax: 762-6400.

Buffalo Lake Naturalists,
Box 1414, Stettler T0C 2L0. Phone: 742-3739.

Calgary Field Naturalists' Society,
Box 981, Calgary T2P 2K4. Phone: 285-8553.

Canadian Parks and Wilderness Society - Edmonton,
11749 Groat Road, Edmonton T5M 3K6.
Phone: 453-8658.

Canadian Parks and Wilderness Society - Calgary,
Box 608, Sub PO 91, University of Calgary,
Calgary T2N 1N4.

Ducks Unlimited Canada - Alberta,
#202, 10470-176 St., Edmonton T5S 1L3.
Phone: 489-2002 Fax: 489-1856.

Edson Bird Club, c/o Alberta Fish and Wildlife,
Suite #108, 111-54 St., Prov. Building, Edson T7E 1T2.

Edmonton Bird Club, c/o Jim Lange,
13216-128 Ave., Edmonton T5L 3H2. Phone: 455-7021.

Edmonton Natural History Club,
Box 1582, Edmonton T5J 2N9. Phone: 484-5788.

Ellis Bird Farm Ltd.,
Box 2980, Lacombe T0C 1S0. Phone: 346-2211.

Federation of Alberta Naturalists,
Box 1472, Edmonton T5J 2N5.
Phone: 453-8629. Fax: 453-8553.

Fort Saskatchewan Naturalists' Society,
c/o 10215-107 St., Ft. Saskatchewan T8L 2H9.

Friends of Environmental Education Society of Alberta,
#320 9939-Jasper Ave., Edmonton T5J 2X5.
Phone: 421-1497. Fax: 425-4506.

Grasslands Naturalists, Box 2491, Medicine Hat T1A 9G8.

Hinton Naturalists, c/o 110 Seabolt Dr., Hinton T7V 1K2.

Lethbridge Naturalists' Society,
Box 1691, Lethbridge T1J 4K4. Phone: 327-8866.

Peace Parkland Naturalists,
Box 1451, Grande Prairie T8V 4Z2.

Red Deer River Naturalists,
Box 785, Red Deer T4N 5H2. Phone: 347-8200.

Strathcona Natural History Club,
Box 146, Ardrossan T0B 0E0.

Vermillion River Natural History Club,
c/o Stu Heard, Box 1769, Vermillion T0B 4M0.
Phone: 853-8400.

Wainwright Wildlife Conservation Society,
c/o Box 1770, Wainwright T0B 4P0. Phone: 842-5513.

SASKATCHEWAN

Canadian Parks and Wilderness Society - Saskatoon,
Box 914, Saskatoon S7K 3M4.
Phone: 249-0040 or 373-4584.

Ducks Unlimited Canada - Regina,
Box 4465, Regina S4P 3W7.
Phone: 569-0424. Fax: 565-3699.

Saskatchewan Eco-Network,
Box 1372, Saskatoon S7K 3N9.
Phone: 665-1915. Fax: 665-2128.

Saskatchewan Environmental Society,
Box 1372, Saskatoon S7K 3N9.
Phone: 665-1915. Fax: 665-2128.

Saskatchewan Outdoor and Environmental Education
Association, 354 Adolph Cres., Saskatoon S7N 3H7.

Saskatchewan Wildlife Federation,
Box 788, Moose Jaw S6H 4P5. Phone: 692-7772.

Saskatchewan Natural History Society,
Box 4348, Regina S4P 3W6.
Phone: 780-9273. Fax: 781-6021.

LOCAL SNHS SOCIETIES:

Fort Qu'Appelle - c/o Ronald Hooper,
Box 757, Fort Qu'Appelle S0G 1S0.

Hudson Bay - c/o Donald Hooper,
Box 40, Somme S0E 1N0.

Indian Head - c/o Vic Beaulieu,
Box 1213, Indian Head S0G 2K0.

Melfort - c/o Phil Curry, Box 1115, Melfort S0E 1A0.

Moose Jaw - c/o Ed Walker,
1071 Laurier St., Moose Jaw S6H 2W6.

Prince Albert - c/o Carman Dodge,
Box 285, Prince Albert S6V 5R5.

Regina - c/o Box 291, Regina S4P 3A1.

Saskatoon - c/o Sub PO #6,
Box 448, Saskatoon S7N 1R1.

Weyburn - c/o Grace Kurtz,
112-6th Ave., Weyburn S4H 1Y8.

Yorkton - c/o Warren Hjertaas,
510 Circlebrooke Dr., Yorkton S3N 2Y3.

MANITOBA

Brandon Naturalists Society
(formerly Brandon Natural History Society),
c/o Mrs. Vera Shuttleworth,
609 McDiarmid Drive, Brandon R7B 2H6.

Canadian Parks and Wilderness Society - Winnipeg,
25 St. Pierre St., Winnipeg R3V 1J5. Phone: 269-7477.

Ducks Unlimited Canada - Winnipeg,
5 - 1325 Markham Rd., Winnipeg R3T 4J6.
Phone: 269-6960. Fax: 261-7662.

Inter-Mountain Naturalists Society,
Box 398, Dauphin R7N 2V2.

Manitoba Eco-Network,
Box 3125, Winnipeg R3C 4E6.
Phone: 956-1468. Fax: 949-9052.

Manitoba Naturalists Society,
302-128 James Ave., Winnipeg R3B 0N8.
Phone: 943-9029.

Manitoba Wildlife Federation,
1770 Notre Dame Ave., Winnipeg R3E 3K2.
Phone: 633-5967. Fax: 632-5200.

Pinawa Naturalists, c/o Peter Taylor,
Box 597, Pinawa R0E 1L0.

Portage Naturalists, 621 Countess Ave.,
Portage la Prairie R1N 0S7. Phone: 857-7155.

Wildlife Foundation of Manitoba,
Box 124, 1961 McCreary Rd., Winnipeg R3Y 1G5.
Phone: 895-7001.

Wildlife Society - Manitoba Chapter,
Box 206, Station L, Winnipeg R3H 0Z5.
Phone: 895-7001. Fax: 895-4700.

WILDLIFE REHABILITATION CENTRES AND ORGANIZATIONS

ALBERTA

Alberta Society for Injured Birds of Prey,
(Strathcona Raptor Centre), c/o Karl Grantmyre,
51562 Range Rd. 222, Sherwood Park T8C 1H4.
Phone: 922-3024.

Alberta Birds of Prey Centre, c/o Colin Weir/Wendy Slaytor,
2124 Burrowing Owl Lane, Coaldale T0K 0L0.
Phone: 345-4262.

Alberta Bird Rescue Association, c/o David and Kim Allan,
51080 Range Rd 223, Sherwood Park T8C 1G9.
Phone: 922-6103.

Calgary Zoo, Box 3036, Station B, Calgary T2M 4R8.
Phone: 232-9300. Fax: 237-7582.

Medicine River Wildlife Rehabilitation Centre,
Box 115, Spruce View T0M 1V0.
Phone: 346-WILD (9453).

Cathie Monson,
13932-109 Ave., Edmonton T5M 2H2.
Phone: 455-6471.

SASKATCHEWAN

Moose Jaw Wild Animal Park,
Box 370, Sub #1, Moose Jaw S6H 5V0.

Western College of Veterinary Medicine,
Small Animal Clinic, University of Saskatchewan,
Saskatoon S7N 0W0. Phone: 966-7126.

MANITOBA

Manitoba Wildlife Rehabilitation Organization,
Box 242, 905 Corydon Ave., Winnipeg R3M 3S7.
Phone: 832-MWRO (6976).

NATURE CENTRES

ALBERTA

Alberta Birds of Prey Centre,
2124 Burrowing Owl Lane, Coaldale T0K 0L0.
Phone: 345-4262.

Beaverhill Lake Nature Centre,
Box 30, Tofield T0B 2J0. Phone: 662-3191.

Bud Miller All Seasons Park Centre,
c/o City of Lloydminster, 5011-49 Ave.,
Lloydminster, SK S9V 0Y8. Phone: 875-4497.

Helen Schuler Coulee Centre,
910-4 Ave. S, Lethbridge TIJ 0P6. Phone: 320-3064.

Inglewood Bird Sanctuary,
c/o Calgary Parks and Recreation,
Box 2100, Station M, Calgary T2P 2M5.
Phone: 269-6688.

John Janzen Nature Centre,
Box 2359, Edmonton T5J 2R7. Phone: 434-7446.

Kerry Wood Nature Centre,
6300-45 Ave., Red Deer T4N 5H2. Phone: 346-2010.

Muskoseepi Park Pavilion,
c/o City of Grande Prairie,
P.O. Bag 4000, Grande Prairie T8V 6V3.
Phone: 538-0451. Fax: 539-1056.

Police Point Interpretive Centre, c/o Parks Dept.,
580 - 1 St. SE, Medicine Hat T1A 8E6.
Phone: 529-6225. Fax: 527-4798.

Shannon Terrace Environmental Education Centre,
Fish Creek Provincial Park, Box 2780, Calgary T2P 0Y8.
Phone: 297-7827.

Strathcona Wilderness Centre,
Strathcona Recreation, Parks and Culture,
2025 Oak St., Sherwood Park T8A 0W9.
Phone: 922-3939. Fax: 922-6415.

SASKATCHEWAN

Meewasin Valley Authority,
402 3rd Ave. S., Saskatoon S7K 3G5.
Phone: 665-6887. Fax: 665-6117.

Wakamow Valley Authority,
Box 1266 276 Home St. E., Moose Jaw S6H 4P9.
Phone: 692-2717. Fax: 692-8188.

Wascana Centre Authority,
Box 7111, 2900 Wascana Dr., Regina S4P 3S7.
Phone: 522-3661. Fax: 565-2742.

MANITOBA

Fort Whyte Centre for Environmental Education,
Box 124, Winnipeg R3Y 1G5.
Phone: 989-8350. Fax: 895-4700.

GOVERNMENT AGENCIES

Alberta Forestry, Lands and Wildlife,
Main Floor, 9925-108 St., Edmonton T5K 2G6.
Phone: 427-6757. Fax: 422-9558.

Saskatchewan Natural Resources,
3211 Albert St., Rm. 430, Regina S4S 5W6.
Phone: 787-2889. Fax: 787-8280.

Manitoba Department of Natural Resources,
Wildlife Branch, Box 24, 1495 St. James St.,
Winnipeg R3H 0W9.
Phone: 945-7775. Fax: 945-3077.

RARE BIRDS

If you see, or find in your nestbox, a bird that you think is rare or unusual for your area or province, you should contact a provincial authority for identification and/or confirmation.

ALBERTA
Edmonton: Curator of Ornithology,
Provincial Museum of Alberta.
Phone: 453-9100 (toll free through the RITE line).
Calgary: Rare Bird Hotline. Phone: 237-8821.

SASKATCHEWAN
Saskatchewan Museum of Natural History,
Contacts: Dr. Paul James (787-2798) or
Robert Kreba (787-2807).
Regina Bird Alert (for whole province). Phone: 949-2505.

MANITOBA
Chief Curator, Natural History Division,
Manitoba Museum of Man and Nature.
Phone: 956-2830. Fax: 942-3679.

BIRD BANDING

Banding is allowed only under license from the Canadian Wildlife Service and provincial wildlife agencies. If you are interested in banding, contact the Bird Banding Office (c/o National Wildlife Research Centre, Canadian Wildlife Service, Environment Canada, Ottawa, ON, KIA 0E7. Phone: 819- 997-1121) and the appropriate provincial government department.

If you find a dead bird with a band on it, contact your local Fish and Wildlife officer in Alberta, Conservation Officer in Saskatchewan or the Department of Natural Resources if you are in Manitoba. If you are sure about the identification of the species, just report the band number. If the species is unfamiliar to you, submit the bird. If you cannot deliver it immediately, wrap it in plastic and freeze it.

Band numbers can also be sent directly to the Bird Banding Office. Once the band number has been traced,you will be advised of where the bird was banded, who banded it, its age and sex etc. Band recovery information is very important to bird researchers, so your assistance and cooperation will be greatly appreciated.

SUPPLEMENTAL FEEDING

For the most part, secondary cavity nesters are not usually attracted to bird feeding stations. Bluebirds, however, will readily take to offerings of mealworms set out in a dish near the nestbox. They will both eat them and feed them to their nestlings. During inclement weather, this additional food supplement may help the nestlings survive. If bluebirds are caught in early or late snowstorms, they may also be attracted to mealworms or an emergency ration mixture of cage bird pellets, raisins and berries mixed into a base of lard or suet.

Most primary cavity nesters, including woodpeckers, chickadees and nuthatches, will be attracted to seed- and suet-feeding stations. For more information on winter bird feeding, we recommend Ellis Bird Farm's *Winter Bird Feeding - An Alberta Guide* which is available at bookstores throughout Alberta or can be ordered through Ellis Bird Farm Ltd.

PESTICIDES AND CAVITY-NESTING BIRDS

In an attempt to determine what impact pesticides may be having on the reproductive success of prairie birds, the Canadian Wildlife Service (Saskatoon), with support from the Wildlife Toxicology Fund of World Wildlife Fund Canada, established the Prairie Nestbox Monitoring Program in 1990. Volunteers collect data on hatching and fledging success of bluebirds, swallows and wrens on their nestbox trails. These data are then analysed with regard to pesticide use, crop type, weather and other factors.

If you find bird kills of any species that may be the result of pesticides, you are encouraged to submit them for analysis. Contact (as soon as possible) the CWS Pesticides Impact Assessment Biologist, Douglas Forsyth (306-975-4087). For more information or to participate in the program, contact Douglas Forsyth or Louise Horstman (403-939-5858).

SHARING YOUR BACKYARD WITH CAVITY NESTERS

People who share their backyards with woodpeckers commonly complain that the birds sometimes choose the house, instead of a tree, to excavate a cavity or advertise their interest in a mate. The chances are the woodpeckers resort to using houses because there is a lack of dead or dying trees in the area. If the woodpeckers are intent upon using your house, you may be able to discourage them by setting out an owl decoy to frighten them away, by insulating your house's gutters and eaves to reduce resonance, and by suspending netting and/or by tacking a piece of plastic over the drumming or pecking site. Provided there is no safety hazard, the best alternative for both you and the woodpeckers is to leave standing as many dead and dying trees in your neighborhood as possible.

Yellow-bellied Sapsuckers have the unpopular habit of drilling orderly rows of holes (sap wells) in birch or other ornamental trees. The sapsuckers can usually be discouraged if aluminum pie plates are hung in the affected tree, or the afflicted area of the tree is wrapped with newspaper or burlap.

Another problem that cavity nesters face, usually in the spring, is misjudging open chimneys for nesting sites. Many ducks, owls and bluebirds have met their fate trapped in a fireplace or stove. This problem can be avoided if you make sure your chimney is fitted with a spark arrester or enclosed with 13-mm (1/2-in.) chicken wire or hardware cloth.

Every spring, we get several reports of bluebirds attacking their reflections in side mirrors on vehicles or in house windows. Females often fight their phantom rivals more aggressively and persistently than males. It seems that the only way to deter such behavior at vehicles is to cover the mirrors or move the vehicle. Discouraging them from fighting windows is often more difficult. If keeping the curtains closed for a few days does not work, try hanging a large blanket or covering the outside of the window with paper or black plastic until the birds resume normal nesting behavior.

GLOSSARY

Avian – pertaining to birds.

Arboreal – tree-dwelling.

Brood – group of young raised simultaneously by a pair of birds or a single adult.

Brood Patch – area of bare skin that develops on the belly of a bird. This bare skin is placed directly on the eggs during incubation to maximize heat transfer to developing, and on newly hatched young to keep them warm.

Brooding – the behavior by parent birds of sitting on their nestlings to warm, conceal or shade them.

Call – an auditory display that is simpler in structure than a song.

Coniferous tree – evergreen, cone-bearing tree, such as a spruce or pine.

Copulation – the physical act of mating.

Courtship – activities related to attracting a mate and maintaining the pair-bond.

Courtship Feeding – one adult feeding the other of a pair, usually during courtship. This behavior helps maintain pair-bonds and often resurges shortly before the young hatch, apparently preparing the parents to start feeding the young.

Deciduous tree – a tree that loses its leaves at the end of the growing season, such as a poplar or maple.

Diurnal – active during the daytime.

Egg Dumping – when a female lays her eggs in a nest other than her own.

Fecal Sac – excrement enclosed in a mucous sac.

Fledge – the moment of flying at the end of the nestling period.

Fledgling – a young bird that has left the nest but is still dependent on its parents for food.

Incubation – the process of keeping eggs at the right temperature to allow development within the egg.

Incubation Period – the time taken for eggs to develop from the start of incubation to hatching.

Insectivorous – insect-eating.

Juvenile – a hatch-year bird that is capable of caring for itself.

Mandible – either part of a bird's beak.

Molt – the replacement of old feathers by new ones.

Monogamous – being pair-bonded to and mating with only one other individual.

Nestling – a young bird in a nest.

Nocturnal – active at night.

Omnivorous – eats both plants and animals.

Passerine – perching bird.

Parasite – an organism that grows, feeds and is sheltered on or in a different organism and contributes nothing to its host.

Parasitize – to lay eggs in the nest of another species and leave the foster parents to raise the young.

Pair-bond – a bond commitment formed between the male and female of a pair.

Polygamous – mating or pairing with more than one mate at a time.

Predator – an animal that captures and eats another.

Range – the distribution of a species. Home range is an area regularly inhabited by a bird, including both its territory (or territories if nesting and feeding territories are different) and any area not defended against other birds. The home range always includes the territory (may be identical in many species).

Resident – a bird that stays in one area all year-round.

Roosting – to sit, rest or sleep on a perch; often several birds congregating together.

Subadult – a yearling bird (in its second year of life) that has reached breeding age, but has not yet acquired adult plumage.

Song – complex auditory displays that are used to delineate territory and attract mates. Usually performed by the male.

Territory – an area that is defended by a bird against its own and sometimes other species.

INDEX